SPIRITUAL MATURITY

By

J. OSWALD SANDERS

"An Overseas Missionary Fellowship Book"

(formerly China Inland Mission)

MOODY PRESS
CHICAGO

CONTENTS

I

II

3

PART I

THE OVERRULING PROVIDENCE
OF GOD

"And we know that all things work together for good to them that love God, to them who are the called according to his purpose" (Rom. 8:28).

READING: Romans 8:26-30

THIS SENTENCE, interpreted in its context, can bring unlimited comfort and cheer to the Christian in time of testing. With Paul it was a matter of profound conviction: "And *we know* that all things work together for good." No room for question here. He had unwavering confidence in the overruling providence of his God. He believed that "God makes everything turn out for the best" (Scholefield). For him this conviction rendered complaining unthinkable since every event of life was either planned or permitted by God. It made possible of achievement his counsel of perfection, "In everything give thanks." It turned sighing into singing. It was a practical embracing of this truth which enabled him and his companion to sing at midnight even when plans seemed to miscarry and they were immured in a dungeon, with bleeding backs. To him it mattered little whether physical conditions were propitious so long as he knew he loved God and was called according to His purpose. Everything, whether seemingly adverse or advantageous, would certainly turn out for the best. The important question is, do we share Paul's joyous assurance?

Paul couches his statement in such categorical terms that it is impossible to remain neutral in the face of its astounding claim. If it were somewhat qualified or expressed in less dogmatic fashion it would be easier to accept. When faced with devastating sorrows or reverses it sounds rather glib and divorced from the grim reality of experience to say that it is all working together for good. But is it really so? Must its assertion be viewed with secret scepticism or can it be embraced with joyous realism? Interpreted in its context, with full value given to each word, there is no verse in the whole of Scripture which will give such poise and serenity in the midst of tragedy, trial or disappointment.

The key to the interpretation of the central statement, "All things work together for good," is that it must be neither isolated from its context nor divorced from its two conditional clauses—"to them that love God" and "to them that are called according to his purpose." These two clauses determine and limit its application. The simple fact is that all things do not without qualification work together for good for everybody. Nor does this verse claim that they do. Two things are presupposed. First there must be correct *relationship* to God. The beneficiary under the promise is a member of God's family, enjoying and manifesting the family affection. Such a person is persuaded that He who did not spare His own Son would never permit or ordain anything which was not for his ultimate good. Love trusts even when it cannot discern. Then there is *partnership*. He is one of "the called" according to God's eternal purpose and his plans have given way to God's plan. To him it is inconceivable that God's perfect design could be thwarted by anything really adverse to him. God is intermingling all things for his good. With his God, "accidents are not accidental and adversity is not adverse." The conclusion is that God's purpose unfolds to those whom He has called and who love Him in return. The promise has nothing for the man in rebellion against God and out of sympathy with His purposes. It is to the cold heart that this verse becomes a stumbling block. It glows with comfort when the heart is warm with love to God. But to be entitled to the comfort of the verse we must come within the category laid down by Paul.

The question inevitably arises, Can tragedy be good? Is ill-health good? Is bereavement good? Is frustration good? Why does God permit these to strike us? In Paul's day there were four characteristic reactions to adversity. The attitude of the Epicurean was, "Let us eat and drink, for tomorrow we die." The Cynic defied fate to do its worst. The Stoic set his teeth and steeled himself to accept the Divine will. Epictetus wrote: "Have courage to look up to God and say, 'Deal with me as Thou wilt from now on. I am as one with Thee; I am Thine; I flinch from nothing so long as Thou dost think that it is good. Lead me where Thou wilt; put on me what raiment Thou wilt. Wouldst Thou have me hold office or eschew it, stay or flee, be rich or poor? For this I will defend Thee before all men.'"

But in the text Paul epitomized the Christian attitude: not defiance or indifference or even resigned acceptance. The Christian joyously embraces adversity or sorrow, knowing that all things whether propitious or adverse are working together for his highest good.

Four truths full of comfort and encouragement emerge from this verse.

GOD'S PLAN IS BENEFICENT. "All things work together *for good*."

The crux of the problem involved in the practical application of this verse lies in our interpretation of the two words "for good." The "good" promised by God in His long-sighted love may not always seem good and acceptable to us. Indeed His providences sometimes appear disastrous when viewed from a materialistic temporal viewpoint. The good promised by God is *spiritual* rather than temporal, and some time may elapse before we discern its true beneficence.

It took years before the strange providences in the life of Job had their vindication. His afflictions had their rise in the malicious mind of Satan, but Job did not attribute them to blind chance or even to Satanic agency. He expressed his philosophy in the noble words, "The Lord gave and the Lord hath taken away; blessed be the name of the Lord." When taunted by his wife he maintained his confidence in God. "What! shall we receive good at the hand of the Lord, and shall we not receive evil?" His stand of faith was abundantly vindicated by subsequent events. He emerged from his trials enriched and not impoverished. Through Job's cooperation, God took the evil acts of Satan and made them work out for good without in any way condoning the evil.

"We tend to interpret good in terms of animal comfort," writes Vernon Grounds. "If we are exempt from disease, if our bodies are never stabbed by pain, if we always have money in our pockets or reserve in the bank, if we live in modern homes and enjoy the latest luxuries, if we can dress well and take long vacations at the seashore . . . that we consider good. Unfortunately we find ourselves victimized by a materialistic civilization, and despite our Christian faith we subtly equate comfort and goodness. In the same way we tend to equate success with goodness. . . . Or yet again we tend to equate pleasure with goodness. . . . And yet such equations are a million miles removed from Paul's basic teaching. And because all of these are false equations, we have trouble with Romans 8:28. Our failure to grasp Paul's conception of the good, changes what ought to be a soft pillow for our hearts into a hard problem for our heads."

> Whate'er my God ordains is right;
> He taketh thought for me.
> The cup that my Physician gives
> No poisoned draught can be,
> But medicine due,
> For God is true.
> And on that changeless truth I build
> And all my heart with hope is filled.

Few tragedies have highlighted this truth more than the fire at Serampore, India, on March 12, 1812. Within a few moments the sacrificial translation work of years of William Carey and his colleagues went up in smoke. The loss in paper for Bibles was immense. The newly cast Tamil type and Chinese metal type were a total loss. Portions of manuscripts, grammars and dictionaries laboriously compiled perished. William Carey wrote, "Nothing was saved but the presses. This is a heavy blow, as it will stop our printing the Scriptures for a long time. Twelve months' hard labor will not reinstate us; not to mention the loss of property, mss., etc., which we shall scarcely ever surmount."

The loss of manuscripts referred to included portions of nearly all his Indian Scripture versions, all his Kanarese New Testament, two large Old Testament books in Sanskrit, many pages of his Bengali dictionary, all of his Telugu Grammar and much of his Punjabi, and every vestige of his well-advanced Dictionary of Sanskrit, the *magnum opus* of his linguistic life.

But there follows his affirmation of faith in words akin to those of our text. "God will no doubt bring good out of this evil and make it promote our interests." Before the ashes were cold, Carey's colleague, Marshman, wrote that the calamity was "another leaf in the ways of Providence, calling for the exercise of faith in Him whose Word, firm as the pillars of heaven, has decreed that all things shall work together for good to them that love God. Be strong therefore in the Lord. He will never forsake the work of His own hands."

In the midst of this desolating reverse, God's servants' grasp of this truth kept their hearts at peace. "It stilled me into tranquil submission, enabling me to look up and *welcome* God's will," said Marshman. Carey told how he had been hushed by the verse, "Be still, and know that I am God." Ward, the third of the famous trio, was found while the fires were still smoldering, not just submissive, but jubilant.

But how could this possibly be working together for good? It did not take long for the strategy of God to appear. "The catastrophe unstopped the ears of British Christendom. In the blaze of the fire they saw the grandeur of the enterprise; the facts were flashed out. And thus the destruction proved a beacon, and multiplied the Mission's zealous friends." So loud a fame it brought them as to reverse the nature of their risks. "The fire has given your undertaking a celebrity which nothing else could," wrote Fuller in a faithful warning. "The public is now giving us their praises. Eight hundred guineas have been offered for Dr. Carey's likeness! If we inhale this incense, will not God withhold His blessing, and then where are we?"

Then what is the nature of the good which Paul had in view? The answer is found in the context: "For whom he did foreknow he also did predestinate *to be conformed to the image of his Son*" (Rom. 8:29). Paul's conception was that anything which made him more like Christ was good, altogether irrespective of its reaction on his comfort or health or success or pleasure. Christlikeness does not always thrive in the midst of material comforts. Many of the most Christlike Christians have been plagued with ill-health. Success in business has in many lives been the death knell of holiness. Seeking after pleasure often defeats its own ends.

GOD'S PLAN IS ACTIVE. "All things *work* together for good."

The heart that loves God discerns Him busily at work in even the most heartbreaking and unwelcome happenings of life. All things are turning out for the best because God is at work in them, transmuting bane into blessing and tragedy into triumph. His operation is not always clearly discernible. Indeed it not infrequently seems that He is doing nothing. Carlyle, meditating on the enigmas of life, in the anguish of his heart said, "The worst of God is that He does nothing." But God is often most active when all seems most still. The working of God in nature is unseen but none the less effective. Under His invisible control the stars maintain their predestined courses, the restless ocean keeps within its appointed limits. We should never, in impatience at the seeming inactivity of God, take things into our own hands and try to be our own Providence.

The daily happenings, whether tragic or joyous, are the raw material from which God is weaving the design of life. "This dance of plastic circumstance, machinery just meant to give the soul its bent." Introduce God into the events of life and order emerges from chaos. "He is too kind to do anything cruel, too wise ever to make a mistake." No conceivable circumstances could better prosper God's plan or further our highest good.

GOD'S PLAN IS INCLUSIVE. "*All* things work together for good."

"All things" means exactly what it says. Everything in every sphere is under the beneficent control of God. It is the comprehensiveness of this statement which is so breathtaking. Bereavement, illness, disappointment, blighted hopes, nervous disorders, children who are giving concern, lack of fruit in service despite earnest endeavor to fulfil conditions of fruitbearing—surely these are not working together for good. Paul quietly asserts that such is the case. We may be willing to admit that life as a whole is subject to the overruling providence of God, but hesitate to believe that every detail of life is the object of His loving concern. Yet our Lord asserted this to be the case. Even the sparrow did not fall to the ground without His Father's knowledge. The circumstances of the Christian's life are ordained of God. There is no such thing as chance. Love refuses to believe that God is not interested in every detail of life. Everything is permitted and designed by Him for wise purposes. He will not cease His supervision for a moment.

Every adverse experience when rightly received can carry its quota of good. Bodily pain and weakness cause us to feel our frailty. Perplexity reveals our lack of wisdom. Financial reverses point up how limited are our resources. Mistakes and failure humble our pride. All these things can be included in the term "good."

GOD'S PLAN IS HARMONIOUS. "All things *work together* for
good."

They work into a preconceived pattern. The events of life
are not unrelated. The physician's prescription is compounded of a number of drugs. Taken in isolation, some of
them would be poisonous and would do only harm. But
blended together under the direction of a skilled and experienced physician they achieve only good. Barclay renders the verse: "We know that God intermingles all things
for good for them that love Him." The experiences of life
when taken in isolation may seem anything but good but
blended together the result is only good.

In adverse circumstances unbelief queries, "How can this
be working for good?" The answer is, "Wait until the Great
Physician has finished writing the prescription." Who cannot look back on life to see that things considered disastrous
proved in the ultimate to be blessings in disguise? The
artist blends colors which to the unskilled eye seem far removed from his objective. But wait until he has finished
his mixing.

Life has been likened to an elaborate tapestry being
woven on the loom. For the beauty of the pattern it is imperative that the colors must not be all of the same hue.
Some must be bright and beautiful, others dark and somber.
It is as they are all worked together that they contribute
to the beauty of the pattern.

> Not until each loom is silent
>   And the shuttles cease to fly
> Will God unroll the pattern
>   And explain the reason why;
> The dark threads are as needful
>   In the Weaver's skillful hand,
> As the threads of gold and silver
>   For the pattern He has planned.

In time of severe trial there is always the temptation,
while assenting to the truth in general, to feel that our

present circumstances are an exception. If that were so, the text is null and void, and the truth of the overruling providence of God in the affairs of men has no meaning. As tragedy upon tragedy overwhelmed Joseph—banishment from home, sale as a slave, unjust imprisonment—it was difficult for him to see these untoward events working together for his good. Yet in retrospect he said to his brothers, "But as for you, ye thought evil against me; *but God meant it unto good*" (Gen. 50:20).

In the events of life, "God has an end in view which is worthy of Him, and will command our fullest approbation when we cease to know in part." Even if called upon to face the wrath of man or Devil we can confidently rest in the assurance that it will ultimately praise God, and that which cannot do so will be restrained.

> Whate'er my God ordains is right;
>   My Light, my Life is He,
> Who cannot will me ought but good;
>   I trust Him utterly:
>   For well I know
>   In joy or woe
> We soon shall see, as sunlight clear,
>   How faithful was our Guardian here.

THE PROSTRATING VISION OF GOD

"I beseech Thee, show me Thy glory" (Exodus 33:18).

READING: Exodus 33:11-23

THIS PRAYER OF MOSES has re-echoed down the centuries. Successive generations of Christians have prayed for a vision of God, often without realizing the possible implications of such a petition. Not infrequently they have failed to recognize the answer when it was granted. John Newton, converted slavetrader, passionately longed for the transforming vision, but the answer to his urgent prayers came in a way which staggered and almost overwhelmed him. He has recorded this experience.

I asked the Lord that I might grow
In faith and love and every grace,
Might more of His salvation know
And seek more earnestly His face.

'Twas He who taught me thus to pray,
And He, I trust, has answered prayer;
But it has been in such a way
As almost drove me to despair.

I thought that in some favored hour
At once He'd answer my request
And by His love's constraining power,
Subdue my sins and give me rest.

Instead of that, He made me feel
The hidden evils of my heart,
And bade the angry powers of hell
Assault my soul in every part.

Nay more, with His own hand He seemed
Intent to aggravate my woe,

14

Crossed all the fair designs I schemed,
  Blasted my gourds, and laid me low.

"Lord, why is this?" I trembling cried.
  "Wilt Thou pursue this worm to death?"
"This is the way," the Lord replied,
  "I answer prayer for grace and faith.

"These inward trials I employ
  From self and sin to set thee free,
And cross thy schemes of earthly joy
  That thou might'st find thy all in Me."

When we pray for a vision of God, what are we expecting?
A glowing vision in the sky? A blinding flash of glory such
as overwhelmed Saul of Tarsus? A thrilling, overpowering
sense of spiritual exaltation? A study of the visions of God
recorded in Scripture gives quite a different picture. In
not one case did the vision immediately result in elation and
ecstasy. With absolute consistency it produced in those to
whom it came profound self-abasement. In every instance
the experience was awe-full, not ecstatic. And the more
intense the vision, the more complete the prostration before
God.

If this is true, before we ask of God a vision of Himself,
we should be prepared for the certain result. In the dazzling whiteness of the snow the cleanest linen appears
soiled. Before the spotless purity and holiness of God,
everything earthly is seen stained and unclean. In the light
of the presence of God, Joshua the holy high priest appeared
"clothed with filthy garments" and therefore disqualified
for office (Zech. 3:1). We have no grounds for expecting
to be exceptions to this rule.

If we ask in what form the vision will come, we are not
left in doubt. "God hath shined in our hearts to give the
light of the knowledge of the glory of God in the face of
Jesus Christ" (II Cor. 4:6). On the canvas of Holy Scripture, with master strokes and in vivid colors the Holy Spirit
has painted the face of Jesus Christ, image of the invisible

God. And it is the same Spirit who will illumine the canvas to the one who longs to see His glory. He has no greater delight than to take of the things of Christ as recorded in His Word and in them to reveal the glory of God.

Although JOB, possibly a contemporary of Abraham, lived in spiritual twilight he had an amazing concept of God and a lofty standard of life. His character was blameless in his own eyes. Conscious of inner integrity he claimed, "I am clean without transgression, I am innocent; neither is there iniquity in me" (33:9). This was not pious cant but the sincere expression of his inner probity. And not only was his character stainless in his own eyes, it was uniquely worthy in God's eyes. Addressing Satan, God asked, "Hast thou considered my servant Job, that there is none like him in the earth, a perfect and an upright man, one that feareth God, and escheweth evil?" (1:8). Few men have enjoyed to such a degree the approval of their own conscience and the commendation of their God.'

Job was one of the very few whom God has called "perfect," thus affirming his blamelessness and integrity. How did this perfect man fare when in the crisis of his mounting trials there came to him the vision of God? He records it in a few pregnant words: "I have heard of thee by the hearing of the ear; but now mine eye seeth thee: Wherefore I abhor myself, and repent in dust and ashes" (42:5-6). *When confronted with the vision of God, the perfect man is reduced to abject self-abhorrence.*

The vision of God was granted to JACOB when, alone at the ford Jabbok, "there wrestled a man with him until the breaking of the day." In naming the spot Peniel, Jacob said with obvious awe: "I have seen God face to face, and my life is preserved" (Gen. 32:24, 30). How did the vision affect Jacob? He was compelled to spell out in terms of his own name, the shame of his character. "And he said unto him, What is thy name? And he said, Jacob"—supplanter, cheat, swindler. Before he could qualify for the blessing

God would bestow on him, he had to confess his true nature. To his dying day he bore the marks of this encounter. *Confronted by the vision of God, the man who had succeeded in deceiving every one else is compelled to acknowledge his own secret shame.*

MOSES could boast of massive learning. He enjoyed the prestige of being called the son of Pharaoh's daughter. His ardent patriotism led him in fleshly impatience to attempt the deliverance of Israel. He would not wait for God to unfold His plan of campaign and in consequence had to hide from the wrath of the king. In the desert his impetuosity turned to passivity, until he was arrested by the Divine vision. "And the Angel of the Lord appeared to him in a flame of fire out of the midst of a bush: and he looked, and, behold, the bush burned with fire, and the bush was not consumed. And God called unto him and said, Draw not nigh hither: put off thy shoes from off thy feet; for the ground whereon thou standest is holy ground. . . . And Moses hid his face; for he was afraid to look upon God" (Exod. 3:2-6). *In the man to whom was to be entrusted the deliverance of God's chosen people, the vision resulted in reverential awe and averted face.*

ELIJAH has been described as the grandest and most romantic character Israel ever produced. He is abruptly projected onto the stage of history in the Carmel drama. And what a man he was! So great was his power with God that he could lock the heavens at will. So little did he fear man that he dared to defy the king, and indeed the whole nation. With Enoch he enjoyed the distinction of entering heaven without passing through the portals of death. How does this dauntless, rugged man of God survive the vision? "And, behold, the Lord passed by, and a great and strong wind rent the mountains . . . and after the wind an earthquake . . . and after the earthquake a fire; but the Lord was not in the fire: and after the fire a still small voice. And it was so, when Elijah heard it, he hid his face in his mantle" (I Kings

19:11-13). *He could remain defiant and petulant in the face
of a majestic display of God's power, but was broken and
subdued by His voice of gentle stillness and hid his face.*

ISAIAH the seer, to whom came the clearest foreshadowing
of gospel truth, was haunted by no sense of inferiority.
Lofty prophecy was mixed with scathing denunciation in
his messages to the nation. He felt perfectly competent to
call down woes on his contemporaries (3:9, 11; 5:8, 11, 20)
until he saw the vision of God. "I saw also the Lord sitting
upon a throne, high and lifted up, and his train filled the
temple. Above it stood the seraphim: . . . And one cried
unto another, and said, Holy, holy, holy, is the Lord of
hosts: the whole earth is full of his glory. And the posts of
the door moved at the voice of him that cried, and the house
was filled with smoke" (Isa. 6:1-5). On whom does he pro-
nounce the next woe after this radiant vision? "Then said
I, Woe is me! for I am undone, because I am a man of unclean lips . . . for mine eyes have seen the King, the Lord
of hosts." *Lips which had mediated the Divine message
were foul and unclean in the light of the holiness of God.*

The vision of God came to EZEKIEL when identified with
his people in their distress and captivity in Babylon. "As I
was among the captives by the river of Chebar . . . the
heavens were opened and I saw visions of God" (1:1)—
visions of God's majesty and omnipresence, of His ceaseless
activity and the glory of His rainbow-circled throne. "And
above the firmament . . . was the likeness of a throne, as the
appearance of a sapphire stone: and upon the likeness of
the throne was the likeness as the appearance of a man above
upon it. . . . And from the appearance of his loins downward
I saw as it were the appearance of fire, and it had brightness
round about it. As the appearance of the bow that is in the
cloud in the day of rain, so was the appearance of the brightness round about. This was the appearance of the likeness
of the glory of the Lord. And when I saw it I fell upon my

face" (1:26-28). *The fearless and faithful seer cannot bear the awful light of the throne on which sits the God of glory.*

Among the saintly men of Scripture, DANIEL is in the front rank. He had held with distinction the post of Prime Minister through the reigns of five successive Oriental despots. That his head remained on his shoulders was remarkable tribute to his wisdom and integrity. His enemies could find no fault in him except that he prayed too much. Of Daniel alone is it recorded that an angelic messenger was sent to tell him how greatly he was beloved by God. Does he emerge unscathed from the beatific vision? Hear his confession: "I, Daniel, alone saw the vision: . . . I was left alone, and saw this great vision, and there remained no strength in me: for my comeliness was turned into corruption, and I retained no strength . . . and when I heard the voice of his words, then I was in a deep sleep on my face, and my face toward the ground" (10:7-9). *One of the most blameless of saints when confronted with the Divine glory is prostrated at the corruption, not of his vices but of his virtues!*

In the midst of an experience of shattering self-revelation a young man wrote: "If I really thought that what I counted to be my prime virtue, my mental honesty, had been so complete a sham as this, I wouldn't be able to go on. And I want to go on. The lesson however is plain. I can't trust myself an inch. Whenever I am most pious, I am probably nursing the most vicious pride. I think it is better to stand at the mouth of the tunnel of personal evil and say, It is infinite . . ."

After a fruitless night's fishing the vision came to PETER, and obedience to Christ's command resulted in a catch which broke the nets. Confronted with this miracle, Peter realized that Christ must either be omniscient in directing them to the shoal of fish, or omnipotent in directing the shoal of fish to them. When he glimpsed the glory of God in the face of Jesus Christ, he was overcome with his own defilement and unworthiness. "Depart from me," he cried, falling down at Jesus' feet, "for I am a sinful man, O Lord" (Luke 5:8). Actually this was the very last thing he wanted, but *when the man whom God would use to open the kingdom to Jew and Gentile saw the vision of God, he could think of no alternative to banishment from His presence.*

SAUL of Tarsus, filled with mistaken zeal for God and lust for the blood of the hated Christians, was making his way toward Damascus. He was proud of the fact that he was a Hebrew of the Hebrews, the strictest of the Pharisees, and was well satisfied with his ardor in the service of God. "Suddenly there shined round about him a light from heaven: and he fell to the earth, and heard a voice saying unto him, Saul, Saul, why persecutest thou me? And he said, Who art thou, Lord? And He said, I am Jesus . . ." (Acts 9:3-5). *The glory of God shining in the face of the ascended Christ blinded and prostrated the man who probably came nearer than any other to justification by works.*

JOHN the beloved was without doubt the sweetest and ripest saint of his day. He was the object of the special love of Christ, not on the grounds of favoritism but because he, more than any of the other disciples, appropriated it for himself. He alone was faithful in the judgment hall. Tradition bears abundant testimony to the charm of his personality and the purity of his devotion to Christ. In the ripe maturity of his old age he is granted the supreme vision of Christ. "I saw one like unto the Son of man . . . His head and his hairs were white like wool . . . his eyes were as a flame of fire . . . his voice as the sound of many waters . . . and his countenance was as the sun shineth in his strength" (Rev. 1:13-17). Surely if anyone is qualified to see the vision of God without being prostrated it will be this man who repeatedly pillowed his head on the bosom of incarnate Deity. Not so. "And when I saw him," John wrote, "I fell at his feet as dead." *Earth's sweetest and most gracious saint falls as though lifeless in the presence of the transcendent majesty and holiness of God.*

A consistent pattern appears throughout these visions. First the vision, then self-abhorrence, self-abasement, the averted face, the sense of uncleanness, blindness, prostration, comeliness turned into corruption, self-banishment, falling as dead. Do we still desire to pray for a vision of God?

But there is another side to the picture. God takes no pleasure in seeing His children lie in the dust. If He abases and humbles them, it is only that He may exalt them in due season. Humiliation is not an end in itself, it merely prepares the way for blessing. The open lesson of these visions surely is that God cannot entrust a man with any deep blessing, any important spiritual ministry until there has come a complete collapse of self.

The collapse of Job's self-righteousness was quickly followed by the bestowal of double what he had lost, and the turning of his captivity through his intercessions for his friends. Jacob's vision resulted in a change of character which gave him new power with God and man. The rebuke of Moses' fleshly energy and apathy with consequent loss of self-confidence, prepared him for the enormous task of delivering God's people. After Elijah's deflation he was encouraged by God and recommissioned for further service. Not only were Isaiah's unclean lips purged and his iniquity removed, but he received an enlarged commission. To Daniel, the sense of corruption gave place to joy in the privilege of being the vehicle of Divine revelation. Peter's deep conviction of unworthiness was a most important element in preparing him to become the mighty Pentecostal preacher. The vision marked Paul out as a chosen vessel to carry God's name before kings and Gentiles. The One who raised John from the ground entrusted him with writing the Apocalypse, the book which for two millenniums has been the stay of a church in persecution. Each vision was the prelude to increased personal holiness and an enlarged sphere of service.

True, the vision of God inevitably leads to self-revelation, but always with a beneficent end in view. God does not aim merely to humiliate us. There is no need to fear being brought to an end of ourselves for "the end of self is the beginning of God." Indeed we may welcome the vision of God if our deepest desire is to advance in holiness and to be of the greatest use to Him.

We may have the vision of God whenever we truly desire it, whenever we are willing for what it involves. And when it has been granted, there is no need to remain groveling in the dust abhorring ourselves. If we heartily repent of all that is amiss as it is revealed in the light of God's presence, we too will hear the words which came to Isaiah: "Thy iniquity is taken away and thy sin purged. . . . Go tell this people. . . ."

THE UNDISCOURAGED PERSEVERANCE
OF GOD

"The God of Jacob" (Ps. 46:7)
"Thou worm Jacob" (Isa. 41:14)

READING: Genesis 32:1-32

No TITLE OF GOD is more startling than this—"The God of Jacob." No two characters seem more ill-matched. But no single sentence more strikingly illustrates the undiscourageable perseverance of God.

The doctrine of the perseverance of the saints has always been prominent in Calvinistic theology but its complementary truth has not always received equal emphasis. The perseverance of the saints is possible only because of the perseverance of God. Were it not for this not one of us would be in the Christian race today. Paul had a magnificent confidence in the Divine perseverance. "Being confident of this very thing, that he which hath begun a good work in you will perform it until the day of Jesus Christ" (Phil. 1:6). He directs our eyes from the pettiness and puniness of man to the might and majesty of God. He lifts us out of our own circumscribed circle into the grand sweep of a Divine purpose which cannot fail.

Our God knows no unfinished task. He completes what He begins. Though Israel balked and thwarted Him at every turn, He persisted in His gracious disciplines until His purposes were realized, and in the Hebrew nation all the peoples of the earth were blessed. When one approach failed He adopted another. If one generation refused to respond He patiently began again with the next. Time and again succeeding generations of Israel turned to idolatry until at last the chastening of their final captivity in Babylon forever taught them its folly and futility. Never since has the Jewish nation worshiped idols.

Our Lord's perseverance was one of the unique characteristics of His life. It had been prophesied of Him, "He shall not fail nor be discouraged, till he have set judgment in the earth" (Isa. 42:4). Nor did He. His loved disciples on whom He had pinned His hopes failed Him. To the very last their weakness and selfish ambitions overrode their love for Him. At the hour of His greatest need they all forsook Him and fled. It was not an enemy, but one of His own intimates, who sold Him into the hands of His bitter foes. Yet through it all He did not fail nor was He discouraged, and it was through these very men that He achieved His purpose. He cherished the unshaken confidence that His Father who had begun the good work would consummate it; no purpose of His would ever fail of fulfillment. We too can share this persuasion. We can trust our God to put the finishing touches to His own work.

The Bible record and Christian experience are replete with evidence of the tenacity and tireless patience of God's pursuing love. Francis Thompson fled from God through the years until he became a human derelict sleeping among the down-and-outs on the Thames Embankment in London. It was there that the love of God overtook and mastered him. In his magnificent poem, *The Hound of Heaven,* he interprets this experience.

> I fled Him, down the nights and down the days;
>   I fled Him down the arches of the years;
> I fled Him, down the labyrinthine ways
>   Of my own mind; and in the midst of tears
> I hid from Him, and under running laughter
>   Up vistaed slopes I sped
>   And shot, precipitated
>   Adown Titanic gloom of chasmed fears
> From those strong feet that followed, followed after.

THE GOD OF JACOB

No more luminous illustration of this truth can be found in Scripture than God's pursuit of Jacob and its apogee in the incongruous title, "The God of Jacob." The God of Abraham, father of the faithful? Yes! The God of Moses, who talked with God face to face as a man to his friend? Yes! The God of Daniel, the beloved? Yes! The God of Jacob, the crooked, the grasping, the deceitful, the swindler? A thousand times, No! God would compromise His own character by linking His name with that of Jacob. And yet He has said, "Jacob have I loved. . . . The God of Jacob is thy refuge. . . . Fear not, thou worm Jacob." What is weaker, what is more worthless than a worm? And yet Jacob the worm, Jacob the worthless, subject of the relentless pursuing love of God, becomes a prince, having power with God and men.

THE SOVEREIGNTY OF HIS SELECTION

Had we been seeking a man to head up a nation through which to achieve a high and holy purpose and in whom all nations were to be blessed, Jacob would have been our last choice. Esau the magnanimous, Esau the large-hearted would have been much higher in the list. Who else but God would have chosen a despicable character like Jacob? There is little that is attractive about this greedy, grasping, scheming man—so mean that he took advantage of his brother's extremity to filch not only his earthly inheritance but his spiritual authority. For Esau should have become the spiritual head of the clan on the death of his father.

To do Jacob justice, it should be noted that his parents showed little nobility of character. "Isaac loved Esau because he ate of his venison"—an undisciplined father, mastered by his appetite. Rebekah loved Jacob with an indulgent and ruinous love. She instigated and aided and abetted him in his deceit—an unscrupulous mother, mastered by an unholy ambition for her favorite son. Esau despised the spiritual and lightly relinquished his spiritual prerogatives. Jacob himself was cunning and mean, ready to exploit even his twin brother. Such was the family God selected for the display of His grace.

Heredity was dead against Jacob, but God is not limited by heredity. When His disciples asked Jesus concerning the blind man, "Who did sin, this man or his parents?" Jesus replied, "Neither hath this man sinned, nor his parents: but *that the works of God might be made manifest in [through] him*" (John 9:2, 3). Here is the key to God's selection of Jacob. He chose a worm that He might transform him into a prince.

The warped character of Jacob provides a striking background for the display of God's incomparable grace, and for the revelation of His attitude towards the weakest of His children. If God chose only the strong, the noble, the brilliant for the achievement of His purpose the vast majority of Christians would be disqualified. Paul in his familiar statement could have been justifying God in His selection of Jacob.

> For ye see your calling, brethren, how that not many wise men after the flesh, not many mighty, not many noble, are called: but God hath chosen the foolish things of the world to confound the wise; and God hath chosen the weak things of the world to confound the things that are mighty; and base things of the world, and things which are despised, hath God chosen, yea and things which are not, to bring to nought things that are: that no flesh should glory in His presence (I Cor. 1:26-29).

It is not generally recognized that Jacob was not a youth but a man of probably seventy years of age when he filched Esau's birthright; or that he was probably over eighty when he cheated him of his blessing. True, he lived to be one hundred and forty-seven, but he was a middle-aged man before these inglorious incidents took place. He was no callow youth but a mature man whose life pattern was set, a man who had obviously persisted in his crookedness for half a lifetime. Psychologists would say his character could never be radically changed at such a late hour, but God is not limited by the laws of psychology. He does not despair of us even when we despair of ourselves. His patience is never at an end. His resources are never exhausted.

THE DEPTHS OF HIS DISCERNMFNT

There is an optimism in God which discerns the hidden possibilities in the most unpromising character. He has a keen eye for hidden elements of nobility and promise in an unprepossessing life. He is the God of the difficult temperament, the God of the warped personality, the God of the misfit. Only God saw the prince in Jacob. He has a solution for every problem of personality and temperament. When we surrender our lives into His hands for drastic and radical treatment, He will bring into play all His resources of love and grace.

"Jacob have I loved, but Esau have I hated" (Mal. 1:3; Rom. 9:13) is one of the most perplexing statements of Scripture as it appears to attribute caprice to God. Two facts must be borne in mind. First, though the language sounds harsh to us, the word "hate" did not always carry the full meaning we give it today. Second, the statement as used by both Malachi and Paul referred primarily to nations —Israelites and Edomites, descendants of Jacob and Esau. God's selection of Jacob was not on the grounds of merit or character, for the choice was made while they were still unborn babes (Gen. 25:23). Paul is asserting that God, "in the exercise of His sovereign will has decreed that faith— not heredity or merit—is the eternal principle of sonship. In their national application 'love' and 'hate' are not the ground of election as we understand those subjective feelings. God is not arbitrary in His choice and cannot be charged with favoritism. The emotional terms indicate rather a national function and destiny. Judah, not Edom, was elected for progressive revelation in history."

But there is also a secondary and individual application of

this statement. God's selection of Jacob and rejection of
Esau was the outcome not of caprice but of discernment.
Behind all Jacob's meanness and duplicity there lay a desire
and a capacity for the spiritual. Time and again he did
violence to it but still it persisted. Esau was generous and
large-hearted but behind this attractive exterior lurked a
despising of the spiritual. He was a splendid specimen, pre-
ferring the gratification of sensual desires to the exercise of a
spiritual ministry.

In spite of all his manifest weaknesses and failures, Jacob's desire for the spiritual provided God with a basis
for His continued pursuit and subsequent dealings. For
the Christian oppressed with the sense of his failure, there
is enormous encouragement in this fact. It is human nature
to notice the worst in the character of our fellowmen, but
God is always looking for what is best. He clearly discerns
the deepest spiritual yearnings of our hearts and works toward their realization. All His chastenings have that end
in view. God appeared five times to Jacob. On each occasion He corrected some blunder of His intransigent child
and on each occasion gave him a fresh opportunity.

THE PERSISTENCE OF HIS PURSUIT

The name "Jacob" means supplanter. Behind the word
lies the idea of a determined and relentless pursuer who, on
overtaking a foe, throws him down—the biography of Jacob
in a single word! Jacob met his match and finally capitulated
to the determined and relentless pursuit of the loving God
who threw him at Jabbok. Had God not been undiscourageable in His pursuit, Jacob would never become a prince with
God. He would have remained an unlovely and unloved
schemer. But in His gracious love God followed him re-
lentlessly from his first encounter at Bethel until his final
conquest thirty years later in the same spot. The Divine
pursuit was marked by four crises.

The first Bethel crisis occurred when Jacob filched the
blessing from Esau. After the pangs of his hunger had been
satisfied, Esau began to realize the implications of his twin

brother's despicable action. On discovering that he had fled, the enraged Esau set off in pursuit. Meanwhile Jacob had his first encounter with God. With head pillowed on a stone, Jacob dreamed he saw "a ladder set up on earth and the top of it reached to heaven: and behold the angels of God ascending and descending on it." Then God spoke, giving him absolute though totally undeserved promises of prosperity and protection, with the added assurance that all families of the earth would be blessed in his seed. Filled with awe he cried, "How dreadful is this place! This is none other but the house of God . . . and Jacob vowed a vow"—and forgot it! (Gen. 28:17, 20). But God did not forget.

Next came *the Peniel crisis*. Jacob was now over a hundred years old. He had spent twenty years serving his unscrupulous uncle Laban. It is instructive to note the disciplines to which God subjected Jacob in order to achieve His purpose. He put him with a man more mean, more grasping, more crooked than himself. All these years Jacob spent swindling and being swindled by his uncle. The supplanter was being supplanted, and the cheat, cheated. But it was this grueling discipline which ultimately led to his transformation. Might this be the reason in some lives for uncongenial home circumstances or working conditions? Could this be why some missionary has been placed with a difficult fellow-worker? We would always choose pleasant conditions and congenial people with whom to work and live, but God is more concerned with our spiritual growth than with our temporal comfort.

It is reassuring to see that God was with Jacob through the whole of this experience and blessed him. He did not permit Laban to do him any injury (Gen. 31:7, 24, 29). Neither will our Laban ever do us any harm. To Jacob's credit be it said that he did not run away from his testing until God's time came. We are apt to chafe at our adverse circumstances and endeavor to evade them but it will always be to our spiritual loss if we short-circuit the Divine disciplines. God will remove them when they have achieved their appointed purpose. Our characters are perfected and enriched by the difficult people and difficult things of life.

While on his way home Jacob learned that Esau was on his way to meet him. Immediately fear begotten of a guilty conscience gripped him. Instead of calling on God and claiming His promised protection (Gen. 28:15), Jacob resorted to carnal scheming and sent carefully prepared and well-spaced gifts to pacify his brother. But the relentless pursuit of God continued. "And Jacob was left alone, and there wrestled a man with him until the breaking of the day."

It was God who began the wrestling match, not Jacob, but Jacob had remarkable powers of resistance. Apparently he thought he could get away with it as he had previously done. But the persistent pressure continued. It is a serious thing to resist a God who is intent to bless. When He found Jacob would not yield, God lamed him. Ever after he bore the marks of that terrible encounter. When he no longer had strength to resist, Jacob wrapped his arms around the Wrestler and refused to let Him go until he received the blessing. As though this was not the point to which God had been working for a lifetime!

> Come O Thou Traveler unknown,
>   Whom still I hold but cannot see;
> My company before is gone,
>   And I am left alone with Thee.
>   With Thee all night I mean to stay,
>   And wrestle till the break of day.
>   —C. WESLEY

Before the blessing could be bestowed there had to be a collapse of the strong self-life of Jacob. He had to face up to the sin and shame of his own character. "What is thy name?" God asks him. "My name is Jacob"—supplanter, cheat, deceiver, confesses the now contrite penitent, and that confession was the distilled essence of a lifetime of failure. Sincerity is ever the precursor of blessing and Jacob had now taken true ground before God. For him, Peniel, "the face of God," meant a confession of utter sinfulness and a consciousness of utter weakness. "I have seen God face to face and my life is preserved," he said with awe. It was at Peniel, too, that he received a further promise of blessing. "Thy name shall be called no more Jacob, but Israel," a prince of God, "for as a prince hast thou power with men and with God, and hast prevailed" (Gen. 32:28). He had prevailed by capitulating. God had succeeded in breaking his hardness. "Yea, he had power over the angel, and prevailed: he wept, and made supplication unto him" (Hos. 12:4).

Now that God had taken away his old name of shame, one would expect Jacob to live up to his new name. But no! He was as suspicious and scheming as ever. These ingrained qualities of his character died hard. Indeed they brought him to *the shameful and sordid Shechem crisis*. Actuated by fear of Esau, he did not complete his journey home but pitched his tent toward Shechem. Like his relative Lot, who was guilty of a similar act of folly at Sodom, he paid dearly for his act of unbelief. Tragedy engulfed his whole family because he would scheme his way out of trouble instead of trusting the God who had twice appeared to him. The subsequent story is one of rape and murder and fear. It is a costly thing to forget a vow or to withdraw a surrender.

Thirty years had elapsed since God first arrested him. Without doubt He would have been justified in abandoning so stubborn and rebellious a character. But God is not man. His love does not blow hot and cold. Instead of abandoning him, He graciously visited him again. "Arise, go up to Bethel, and dwell there: and make there an altar unto God, that appeared to thee" (Gen. 35:1). This was the *second Bethel crisis*.

This time the disciplines of God over thirty years had done their work. Jacob did not linger. Immediately he gathered his family and hastened to Bethel. "And God appeared unto Jacob *again* . . . and blessed him." God is utterly undiscourageable in His purpose to bless His people. Once more Jacob heard the words, "Thy name shall not be called any more Jacob, but Israel shall be thy name: and He called his name Israel" (Gen. 35:9, 10). This time Jacob lived up to the privileges of his new name and did not backslide into his former scheming and deception. The disciplines of God had been effective and Jacob the worm finds his way into God's gallery of men of faith in Hebrews 11. "Where sin abounded, grace did much more abound."

There is no fundamental difference between one man and another. Only the incidence of temptation is different. In face of onslaughts of the common temptations such as jealousy, pride, ambition, money, or sex, the great majority of people commonly experience failure. They fall far below their own ideals. The same old sin revives, gathers strength and masters them. The same tragic failure or flaw in character pursues them throughout life like a bloodhound. Paralysis of hope develops through a succession of defeats.

The Devil preaches a message of despair. But in the typical life of Jacob, God is preaching the gospel of recovery. The laws of heredity are not the highest laws. The God of Jacob is pre-eminently the God of the second chance to Christians who have failed and failed persistently. The second chance does not avert the consequences of past failure, but even failure can be a steppingstone to new victories. To the child of God failure can have an important educative value. God does not waste even failure.

The outstanding lesson of Jacob's life is that *no failure need be final.* There is hope with the God of Jacob for any disposition or any temperament. No past defeat puts future victory out of reach. When God has saved and apprehended a man, He pursues him with undiscourageable perseverance that He may bless him. He does not exclude from His royal service penitent men who have failed. Had God dismissed Peter for his failure, there would have been no great Pentecostal preacher. God will turn the tables on the Devil by creating a wider ministry out of our very defeats.

THE DISCRIMINATING DISCIPLINES
OF GOD

"Doth the plowman plow continually to sow?" (Isa. 28:24)

READING: Isaiah 28:23-29

LET HIM PLOW, He purposeth a crop." This reaction of Samuel Rutherford to the chastenings which came to him, revealed a true insight into the Divine disciplines and an attitude calculated to benefit most from them. The disciplines of life may be painful but they are never purposeless. "I grant that all chastening considered in the light of the immediate present, seems to be fraught not with pleasure, but with pain; but in the long run it yields *a harvest of peace* to those who have been disciplined by it, *a harvest of righteousness*" (Heb. 12:11, Way). If we desire the harvest, we must welcome the discipline.

The paragraph under consideration occurs in one of Isaiah's greatest prophecies. "It is distinguished by that regal versatility of style which places its author at the head of the Hebrew prophets. Keen analysis of character, realistic contrasts between sin and judgment, clever retorts and epigrams, rapids of scorn and a spate of judgment—but the final issue, a placid stream of argument baulked by sweet parable" (G. A. Smith). This "sweet parable" uses the methods of the farmer as typical of God's dealings with the nations and, in a secondary application, with the church and its individual members.

Isaiah highlights those qualities in God which give Him such a sure touch in His dealings with men. "For his God doth instruct him to discretion, and doth teach him" (v. 26).

"The Lord of hosts . . . wonderful in counsel, and excellent
in wisdom" (v. 29). He is no mere experimenter in lives.
He is moved neither by caprice nor prejudice. Every activity is dictated by the highest wisdom and executed in
the deepest love. And through it all there is an exquisite
discernment and discrimination. The means adopted are always those best suited to attain the end in view. Rightly
received, an abundant harvest is assured.

The skill of the farmer, his careful judgment in the three
main processes of husbandry—plowing, sowing, harvesting—
is but a reflection of the skill and wisdom of the God who
instructed him. If the farmer shows such keen discernment
and exercises such careful oversight of his crops, Isaiah ar-
gues, will the God who counseled him be less discriminating
in the much more delicate task of producing a harvest from
our lives?

THE DISCRIMINATION OF HIS DISCIPLINES

Although the heavenly Husbandman permits the plowshare and harrows of sorrow or suffering to tear through
the lives of His children, they are always guided and controlled by a supremely skillful hand. His ultimate purpose,
a harvest, is ever kept in view. The three principal processes
of farming are employed by Isaiah to illustrate the wisdom
God exercises in His character-training and tempering of the
spirit.

Viewing the successive operations of plowing, sowing
and threshing as suggestive of the disciplines of life, three
truths emerge from this parable.

God is discerning in their duration. "Does he who plows
for sowing plow continually? Does he continually tear up
and harrow his land?" (vv. 23, 24). Of course he does not.
"His God doth instruct him to discretion and doth teach
him" (v. 26). Plowing is only a means to an end. When the
end is achieved his plowing ceases. In the history of Israel
God's discernment can be seen. For four hundred and thirty
years the plow of the Egyptian tyranny ripped through the

stiff soil of the Hebrew nation, an unpromising wilderness in which God saw possibilities of a rich harvest. But there could be no harvest without plowing. As soon as the discipline of the Egyptian taskmaster's whip had achieved its purpose it was removed. Not one day longer than was necessary to achieve the beneficent Divine purpose did He permit His people to writhe under the oppression of their masters. As soon as they were ready to receive deliverance He led them into the rest and abundance and victory of Canaan. But only the severity of the discipline weaned them from Egypt.

The skillful farmer discriminates between one soil and another. Light and sandy soil requires only brief and light plowing. Stiff, sour clay requires totally different treatment if it is to produce a crop. It must be laid bare to the sun and drained. The plow must plunge deep into the subsoil, as deep as the share will go. Soil must be harrowed and harrowed again until the clods are broken down and a fine tilth secured in which the precious seed will germinate and grow. The farmer is discerning in the duration of his plowing. He does not continually tear up and harrow his land. He deals with each soil according to its need. Is not this the explanation of the differing incidence of suffering and sorrow and trial? The heavenly Husbandman can be trusted in the adaptation and timing and duration of the disciplines His love permits. We are safe in His hands.

The discipline is always preparatory to blessing and can bring nothing but blessing when rightly received. It is here that our responsibility lies. Food not digested is a bane, not a blessing. Disciplines not rightly received sour rather than sweeten the character. To querulously ask "Why?" when the chastening stroke falls is in effect to charge the all-wise and all-loving God with caprice. He does not rend the heart merely to demonstrate His power and sovereignty but to prepare for greater fruitfulness. He prunes every branch that does bear fruit to increase its yield. The discipline is purposeful. How do we react to God's plow? Does it soften,

subdue, chasten us? Or does it harden and stiffen our resistance to His will? Does it sweeten or sour us?

Our reaction to family problems and financial reverses,
to suffering and disappointment, to thwarted ambitions and
disappointed expectations is all-important. If we submit,
feeling that resistance is unavailing, that is better than continued rebellion. If we acquiesce in God's dealings, although without joy, that is higher ground. But it is when
we embrace God's unexplained providences with a song that
God is most glorified and we are most blessed. When Samuel
Rutherford lay in Aberdeen prison, he used to write at the
top of his letters, "God's Palace, Aberdeen."

Madame Guyon, a cultured Frenchwoman, was imprisoned for her faith from 1695 to 1705. Instead of repining
at her lot, she joyously accepted God's will as her weal.
"While I was a prisoner in Vincennes," she wrote, "I passed
my time in great peace. I sang songs of joy which the maid
who served me learned by heart as fast as I made them.
And we together sang Thy praises, O my God. The stones
of my prison walls shone like rubies in my eyes. My heart
was full of that joy which Thou givest to them that love
Thee in the midst of their greatest crosses." It was here she
wrote one of her choicest hymns.

> A little bird am I
>   Shut out from fields of air,
> Yet in my cage I sit and sing
>   To Him who placed me there,
> Well pleased a prisoner to be,
> Because, my God, it pleaseth Thee.
>
> Naught else have I to do,
>   I sing the whole day long,
> And He whom most I love to please
>   Doth listen to my song.
> He caught and bound my wandering wing,
> But still He bends to hear me sing.

My cage confines me round,
  Abroad I cannot fly,
But though my wing is closely bound,
  My heart's at liberty.
My prison walls cannot control
The flight, the freedom of the soul.

O, it is good to soar
  These bolts and bars above,
To Him whose purpose I adore,
  Whose providence I love,
And in Thy mighty will to find
The joy, the freedom of the mind.

Job experienced the tearing of the plowshare through his life, but his reaction silenced the adversary who designed to make capital against God out of his failure. Satan had no answer to Job's noble statement, "The Lord gave, the Lord hath taken away; blessed be the name of the Lord." God's confidence in Job was abundantly vindicated.

"These little troubles (which are really so transitory) are winning for us a permanent and glorious reward out of all proportion to our pain. For we are looking all the time not at the visible things but at the invisible. The visible things are transitory. It is the invisible things that are really permanent" (I Cor. 4:17-18, Phillips). It is when we turn our eyes away from the immediate and fix them on the ultimate that we are able to correctly interpret the disciplinary experiences of life.

He is careful in their choice. "Does He not rather, after leveling the surface scatter the dill and sow cummin, put the wheat in rows, barley in the appointed places, and rye around the border? His God correctly instructs and teaches him" (vv. 24-26, Berkeley Version). The prudent farmer exercises the finest discrimination both in the evaluation of his seeds and in the selection of their situation. He is not haphazard in his methods. The more valuable seeds are given the most favorable position. The less valuable can fill in waste corners. Dill and cummin are small seeds used as a

relish and therefore comparatively unimportant when compared with the essential wheat and barley. The farmer is always calculating what will pay him best and how he can
get the maximum return from his land.

So it is with God. He never wastes His disciplines. He
knows which will produce the most luxurious harvest. Each
is carefully selected by infinite wisdom. He regards our
lives as the seed plots of eternity and pays attention not
only to the seed but to the soil. The incidence and timing
of His corrective dealings are meticulously correct. He who
correctly instructs and teaches the farmer does not exercise
less wisdom in His culture of a human heart. His selection
is unerring, whether it be delay or denial, withholding or
withdrawing, prosperity or adversity, joy or suffering. He
always has a crop in view.

Are we less prudent than the farmer in our assessing of
relative values and in deciding priorities? It is in this that
success, both temporal and spiritual, lies. We reap what we
sow. If the soil of our lives is sown with the trivial and the
carnal, they will produce after their own kind. If on the
other hand we sow the primary and the spiritual, there will
be an abundant harvest of holiness and joy.

He is considerate in their moderation. "For the fitches are
not threshed with a threshing instrument, neither is a cart
wheel turned about upon the cummin; but the fitches are
beaten out with a staff, and the cummin with a rod. Bread
corn is bruised; because he will not ever be threshing it,
nor break it with the wheel of his cart, nor bruise it with
his horsemen. This also cometh forth from the Lord of
hosts, which is wonderful in counsel, and excellent in working" (Isa. 28:27-29). The farmer has regard to the nature of
the seed as well as its value and adapts his threshing tech-
nique accordingly. To treat each seed alike would irrepar-
ably damage some or leave others unseparated from the
husk. He must apply exactly the correct length of time to
achieve the end in view. Gentle tapping with a rod is sufficient for the dill but the wheat requires the *tribulum,* a

heavy threshing-sledge. His intelligence and experience prevents the farmer from excess in his threshing method. As soon as the seed is separated from the restricting husk, the threshing process ceases.

God exercises a similar discretion and moderation in the methods He adopts to produce the harvest in the lives of His children. He does not use the heavy *tribulum* (from which our word "tribulation" is derived) where a light rod would achieve His purpose. His object is not the crushing, the destruction of the grain, but its purification and preservation. If He sends tribulation it is because no other means will produce the result. He employs no more force and for no longer than is necessary. Fruitfulness is the end of all discipline. True spirituality welcomes tribulation if it will produce a richer harvest for God. "I glory in tribulation," said Paul, and he certainly knew what he was speaking of. Never was nature more sensitive than his, but seldom has a man experienced more of the chastening rod.

THE PURPOSE OF GOD'S DISCIPLINES

There is infinite variety in the dealings of God both in their character and their incidence. No two people are treated alike by Him. He recognizes the uniqueness of personality and this is reflected in His disciplinary method.

God's dealings have a threefold purpose.

Personal—to cultivate the soul. What we are is much more important than the amount we do. God is supremely concerned with the development of Christlike character. He purposes that every Christian should be "conformed to the image of his Son." Even His Son could be brought to maturity in the human experience necessary for His office as High Priest only through suffering. There is no substitute. Where discipline is not applied, or goes unheeded, there is no harvest of personal holiness and likeness to Christ.

It is recorded that when in His grace the Lord lavished kindness upon His people, the response was not gratitude but rebellion. "He made him to ride on the high places of the earth . . . and he made him to suck honey out of the rock and oil out of the flinty rock; butter of kine, and milk of sheep, with fat of lambs . . . with the fat of kidneys of wheat. . . . But Jeshurun waxed fat, and kicked" (Deut. 32:13-15).

Character is often unevenly developed. "Ephraim is a cake not turned," said Hosea; a cake well done on one side and undercooked on the other. God is not content with a partial sanctification, with Christians who are overdeveloped in some respects but deficient in others. It is to correct this inequality that He applies the fires of testing to the underdeveloped side of our characters.

Relative—to provide food for others. "Bread corn is bruised" is the Authorized Version rendering, and this is without doubt true, but it is not bruised in the threshing process or it would lose its value. The A.S.V. is probably more accurate in its text. "Bread grain is ground; for he will not be always threshing it" (v. 28). The farmer does not needlessly crush the grain with the *tribulum.* Grain in the husk is useless for human consumption and the objective of threshing is to separate the grain from the husk, so that the grain may be ready for consumption. Once it is threshed, it goes through the bruising and grinding process.

> Bread corn is bruised! Shrink not, my soul,
> From the plucking and the binding,
> From the break and the grind:
> The heart God breaks, He doth make whole.
> The corn unshelled and thrown aside
> Cannot for man's sore need provide.

Our Lord was "bruised for our iniquities" that He might become to us the Bread of Life to sustain us. "A disciple is not above his master, nor a servant above his lord. It is enough for the disciple that he be as his master, and the servant as his lord" (Matt. 10:24, 25). We should not wonder, then, that bruising is the price of a spiritual ministry.

Ultimate—to prepare for Heaven. This life is but the kindergarten of Heaven and God would have us master the elementary spiritual lesson that where there is no cross, there can be no crown. Where the yoke is not taken, the rest is not enjoyed. But we are slow scholars and the lesson has often to be learned over and over again.

"We cease to wonder so much at the care God takes of human character," wrote Alexander Whyte, "and the cost He lays out upon it, when we think that it is the only work of His hands that shall last forever. It is fit, surely, that the ephemeral should minister to the eternal, and time to eternity, and all else in this world that shall endure or survive this world; all else we possess or pursue shall fade and perish, our moral character shall alone survive. Riches, honor, possessions, pleasures of all kinds; death with one stroke of his desolate hand shall one day strip us bare to a winding sheet and a coffin of all the things we are so mad to possess."

THE PERFECTED STRENGTH OF GOD

"My strength is made perfect in weakness" (II Cor. 12:9)

READING: I Cor. 1:25–2:5; II Cor. 12:7-10

THERE IS AN ARRESTING DIFFERENCE between God's thoughts and man's concerning weakness and inadequacy. We are inclined to consider these justifiable excuse for shrinking from the difficult task. God advances these very qualities as reasons for tackling it. We maintain that we are too weak. God asserts that to be the very reason He chose us. Instead of the wise and mighty and noble filling the front ranks of God's army, we find the foolish, the weak, the despised, the nonentities. And why? That no human being might boast in the presence of God, and that His strength might be made perfect in our weakness. "Ye see your calling, brethren, how that not many wise men after the flesh, not many mighty, not many noble, are called: but God hath chosen the foolish things of the world to confound the wise; and God hath chosen the weak things of the world to confound the things that are mighty; and base things of the world, and things which are despised, hath God chosen, yea, and things which are not, to bring to nought things that are" (I Cor. 1:26-28).

THE PRINCIPLE INVOLVED

An important spiritual principle is involved, which must be mastered by all who wish to be their best for God. God is not confined to the greatly gifted and exceptionally clever for the fulfillment of His purposes. Indeed, He can use them only as they abandon reliance on their purely natural

42

abilities. All through history God has chosen and used non-entities because their unusual dependence on Him left room for the unique display of His power. When they are content to be nothing, He can be everything. He chooses and uses the richly endowed only when they renounce dependence on their own abilities and resources.

Paul does not say in the above paragraph that God did the best He could with the poor material at His disposal. He deliberately chose them, passing by the wise, the mighty, and the noble if they refused to renounce not their gifts and qualifications but dependence on these in attaining spiritual ends. This is surely a challenging and revolutionary thought—God will not use us in spite of our weakness and inadequacy but actually because of them. He refuses to use our most spectacular gifts and unique qualifications until we are weaned from reliance on them. Human weakness provides the best backdrop for the display of Divine power.

An exaggerated emphasis on talents and qualifications has closed the door to the mission field for many a fine potential missionary. "They will offer their services to any society which will guarantee the full employment of their skills," writes L. T. Lyall. "This is necessary to satisfy their families and friends that all the long grind leading up to qualification is not going to be altogether wasted. Surely God must have allowed them to have this training in order to use it! Abraham laid down no such conditions. Nor did Paul. Nor did any of the outstanding missionaries between their day and ours. Most of them allowed their talents to fall into the ground and die, but they became fruitful missionaries. The Lord demands unconditional discipleship. A Christian is under orders. He must not ask to see the path before stepping out on it. It is for us to obey our omniscient Lord and leave it to Him to deploy us where He sees our qualifications can be most strategically employed. The current attitude of requiring assurance that one's qualifications will find adequate outlet may be an evidence of a lack of full surrender to the Lordship of Christ. If we believe God has

given us a special stewardship in our training, can we not
trust Him if it seems that He puts the gifts aside for a time—
or even forever?"

"My strength is made perfect in weakness" was God's
message to Paul. "When I am weak, then am I strong" was
Paul's testimony (II Cor. 12:9, 10). Of God's heroes it is
recorded that it was "out of weakness they were made
strong" (Heb. 11:34).

William Wilberforce, the great Christian reformer who
was responsible for the freeing of the slaves in the British
Empire, was so small and frail a creature that it seemed
even a strong wind might knock him down. But once Bos-
well heard him speak in public in advocacy of his great
cause, and afterwards said, "I saw what seemed to me a
shrimp mount the table, but as I listened he grew and grew
until the shrimp became a whale."

"It is a thrilling discovery to make," writes J. S. Stew-
art, "that always it is upon human weakness and humiliation, not human strength and confidence, that God chooses
to build His kingdom; and that He can use us not merely in
spite of our ordinariness and helplessness and disqualifying
infirmities, but precisely because of them. . . . *Nothing can
defeat a church or soul that takes, not its strength but its
weakness, and offers it to God to be His weapon.* It was the
way of Francis Xavier and William Carey and Paul the apostle. 'Lord, here is my human weakness. I dedicate it to
Thee for Thy glory.' This is the strategy to which there is
no retort. This is the victory which overcomes the world."

THE PRINCIPLE ILLUSTRATED

Our trouble is not that we are too weak but that we are
too strong for God. King Uzziah was "marvelously helped
till he was strong. But when he was strong, his heart was
lifted up to his destruction" (II Chron. 26:15, 16). Jacob
became a prince having power with God and man only after
the sinew of his strength withered under the touch of his

Divine Antagonist. Paradoxical as it may seem, "the lame take the prey" (Isa. 33:23). God calls our hindrances helps, and it is our direst extremity which affords Him His greatest opportunity.

Dwight L. Moody was innocent of formal education. His letters, many of which have been preserved, are full of grammatical errors. His physical appearance was not impressive. His voice was high pitched and his tones nasal. But these handicaps did not prevent God using him to shake two continents. A reporter was sent by his newspaper to cover Moody's campaign in Britain, in which aristocracy and artisan alike turned to God, and to discover the secret of his power. After considerable observation he reported: "I can see nothing whatever in Moody to account for his marvelous work." When Moody read the report, he chuckled, "Why, that is the very secret of the movement. There is nothing in it that can explain it but the power of God. The work is God's, not mine."

> It is a secret joy to find
> The task assigned beyond our powers,
> For thus, if ought of good be wrought,
> Clearly the praise is His, not ours.
>
> —F. HOUGHTON

But God does not confine Himself to the Moodys and Careys of the world. Think how He used Paul the apostle. He could be classed among the wise, the mighty, the noble. He had everything—intellectual power, emotional ardor, irresistible logic, quenchless zeal. But he placed reliance on none of these. "And I, brethren . . . came not with excellency of speech or of wisdom, declaring unto you the testimony of God. For I determined not to know any thing among you, save Jesus Christ and him crucified. And *I was with you in weakness,* and in fear, and in much trembling. And my speech and my preaching was not with enticing words of man's wisdom, but in demonstration of the Spirit and of power" (I Cor. 2:1-4). He had everything, but he renounced dependence on his superb gifts and training, and placed his sole reliance on his adequate God.

Moses, too, illustrates the principle. As the young scholar-prince, he was supremely self-sufficient and attempted singlehanded the deliverance of his oppressed fellows. But he was not yet equipped for God's purpose. He was banished from Egypt to undertake a forty-year course in the university of the desert. So thoroughly did he master the difficult lesson of human weakness that he shrank from the call of God when it came to him. He adduced seven reasons why he should not do God's will, all of them based on his own weakness and incapacity.

His inventory of disqualifications covered lack of capability (Exod. 3:11), lack of message (3:13), lack of authority (4:1), lack of eloquence (4:10), lack of special adaptation (4:13), lack of previous success (5:23), and lack of previous acceptance (6:12). A more complete list of disabilities it would be difficult to conjure up. But instead of pleasing God, his seeming humility and reluctance stirred His anger. "The anger of the Lord was kindled against Moses" (4:14). In point of fact the excuses Moses advanced to show his incapacity were the very reasons for God's selection of him for the task. Now, emptied of self-confidence and self-dependence, Moses would lean on his God.

For each of his disabilities God had a satisfying answer and an appropriate provision. The forgotten factor was that God's call always guarantees God's equipment for the task. His weakness became God's weapon when it cast Moses back on God's illimitable resources. Our "Who is sufficient for these things?" can be merely the despair of unbelief. The joyous response of faith is, "Our sufficiency is of God."

The story of Gideon's victory by the three hundred illustrates the principle from a different angle. In his response to the Divine call Gideon affords a perfect example of conscious inadequacy. "O my Lord, wherewith shall I save Israel? Behold my family is poor in Manasseh, and I am the least in my father's house" (Judges 6:15). But encouraged

by God's promise of victory and confirmatory signs, he
responded to the call. The 32,000 followers who rallied to
his side seemed pitifully inadequate to meet 135,000 Midia-
nites, but they were "too many" for God (7:2). The courage
test eliminated 22,000, but the remaining 10,000 were "yet
too many" (7:4). These were again sifted by the drinking
test which was survived by only 300 eager and disciplined
men. Gideon's band was now outnumbered by 450 to 1.
Instead of arming them with the most potent weapons, God
orders that their weapons shall be fragile pitchers, flaming
torches, and rude trumpets. Had military strategy ever
seemed more absurd? Yet God's picked and obedient men
won the day. "All the host ran and cried and fled" before
them (7:21). Totally inadequate numbers and equipment
were more than compensated for by the omnipotence of
God. The utter weakness of Gideon's band became His
weapon for victory. And the reason for stripping the inadequate Gideon of human resources? "Lest Israel vaunt themselves against me, saying, Mine own hand hath saved me"
(7:2), a reason akin to Paul's, "That no flesh should glory
in his presence" (I Cor. 1:29).

"This is the strategy of God . . . that the world should
know that Christianity—all the triumphs of faith in individual lives and the onward march and mission of the
Church—is not to be explained by anything in man, any
human virtue, prowess, ability (for in the light of the men
involved any such explanation would be absurd). Therefore
the only possible explanation must be supernatural and
Divine."

THE PRINCIPLE VINDICATED

Francis de L. Booth Tucker, a brilliant young officer in
the Indian Civil Service, filled an important post. Rapid
promotion lay ahead of him, but he had met and yielded to
the claims of Christ. Becoming dissatisfied with his self-
centered life, he longed to be able to do more for the morally
and spiritually destitute people around him. He heard of

the recently organized Salvation Army and its tremendous impact on the unprivileged classes in England. He resigned his post and threw in his lot with the new movement. He proceeded to England, and after a period of training returned to India as a Salvation Army missionary. However, despite his most sacrificial efforts, he seemed unable to bridge the gap between him and the needy Indian people. He was failing to achieve the very thing for which he had abandoned his worldly prospects. After much prayer he determined to adopt native dress, take a begging bowl as did their holy men, and live on what the poor people chose to give him.

With a companion he set out on his new venture, traveling barefoot on the burning midsummer roads. Native people who had never worn shoes were inured to the heat, but before long Booth Tucker and his companion found their feet a mass of blisters that made every step an agony. Coming to a village in the heat of the afternoon, they expected at least a drink of water and something to eat but they were denied entry. Thoroughly dispirited, they lay down under a tree and fell asleep. While they slept some of the men gathered around them. One, amazed to see the blisters on their feet said, "How much these men must care for us to suffer in this way to bring us their message. They must be good men and we have treated them badly." When the missionaries awoke, they were invited into the village, their feet were bound up, and food and drink spread before them. Then followed the coveted opportunity of presenting the Gospel message to these members of a criminal tribe. Thus began a movement which swept 25,000 into the kingdom. It was not his undoubted brilliance but his obvious weakness which opened the hearts of the people. When he was weak, then he was strong. His weakness became God's weapon. God's strength was perfected in his weakness.

THE MORAL ANTIPATHY OF GOD

"These six things doth the Lord hate . . . a proud heart"
(Prov. 6:16, 17)

READING: Isaiah 14:12-15; Ezekiel 28:11-19

THE BIBLE DOES NOT TELL how sin entered the universe, but
we are told how it entered our world and that it originated
before it made its presence felt here. It is characteristic of
Scripture revelation that while it does not tell us everything
we would like to know, it tells us all we need to know to
enable us to meet the exigencies of life and to live victorious-
ly over sin and circumstances. To do this, it is not necessary
that we know the primal origin of sin, but it is essential that
we know the nature and character of the fundamental sin
which has blighted the world ever since it was entertained
by our first parents.

In Genesis, the original temptation to sin was presented
by the Devil, who himself had fallen from his lofty position.
Two Old Testament passages throw light on the nature of
his sin (Ezek. 28:11-19 and Isa. 14:12-15), passages which
primarily refer to the king of Tyre and the king of Babylon.
But the meaning of these Scriptures obviously cannot be
exhausted by mere men. The Ezekiel passage runs: "Thou
sealest up the sum, full of wisdom, and perfect in beauty.
Thou hast been in Eden the garden of God; every precious
stone was thy covering. . . . Thou art the anointed cherub
that covereth. . . . Thou wast perfect in thy ways from the
day that thou wast created, till iniquity was found in thee.
. . . and thou hast sinned; therefore I will cast thee as pro-
fane out of the mountain of God. *Thine heart was lifted
up* [was proud] because of thy beauty . . . I will cast thee
to the ground." How reminiscent of the words of our Lord,

49

"I beheld Satan as lightning fall from heaven" (Luke 10: 18).

Or again the Isaiah passage: "How art thou fallen from heaven, O Lucifer . . . for thou hast said in thine heart, I will ascend into heaven, I will exalt my throne above the stars of God. I will sit also upon the mount of the congregation . . . I will ascend above the heights . . . *I will be like the Most High*. Yet thou shalt be brought down to hell."

The historical characters to whom these passages had primary reference could not exhaust the full significance of these extraordinary statements, which without doubt have a deeper meaning. This method of revelation of truth is employed elsewhere in Scripture, *e.g.*, in the Messianic Psalms where the Psalmist, though apparently referring to himself, made statements which in their fulness could refer only to the Messiah (Psalms 2, 22, and 110). This finds confirmation elsewhere in Scripture. So we have grounds for inferring that these passages have a secondary application to Satan, who occupied the lofty office of guardian and protector of the throne of God. He was the daystar, holding a position of unsurpassed glory near the Sun of Righteousness.

What caused his downfall? The fundamental sin of *pride*, the sin of seeking to establish a throne of his own. Instead of guarding the throne of God which he was set to protect, he struck at it and attempted to dethrone the Almighty. Pride led to self-exaltation which expressed itself in self-will. The essence of his sin was that he wanted to be independent of God. Pride is the self-sufficiency of a selfish spirit that desires only unrestrained independence. "*I* will set *my throne* on high. . . . *I* will make *myself* like the Most High." This is the fundamental sin which tries to enthrone *self* at the expense of God.

Though Satan was cast down, in his fall he wrested the scepter of sovereignty of the world from man and now rules as god of this world. In Eden he sowed the seeds of the same tragic sin. "In the day ye eat thereof . . . ye shall be as gods" (Gen. 3:5) he promised. Compare this with his "I will make myself like the Most High." Satan fell through pride. Adam and Eve fell through pride and implicated the whole human race in their ruin. You and I fall through pride, the fundamental sin which lies at the root of every other sin, the desire to be master of our own lives and to be independent of God. Since this is so, it is little wonder that pride leads the list in every catalog of sins compiled by the church.

GOD'S ANTIPATHY TO PRIDE

No sin is more hateful and abhorrent to God. Sins of the flesh are revolting and bring their own social consequences, but against none of those does God speak with such vehemence as He does of pride.

"Him that hath . . . a proud heart will I not suffer [endure]" (Ps. 101:5).

"The proud he knoweth afar off" (Ps. 138:6).

"These six things doth the Lord hate; yea, seven are an abomination unto him: . . . a proud look" (Prov. 6:16, 17).

"Pride . . . do I hate" (Prov. 8:13).

"Every one that is proud in heart is an abomination to the Lord" (Prov. 16:5).

"Pride goeth before destruction, and a haughty spirit before a fall" (Prov. 16:18).

"A proud heart . . . is sin" (Prov. 21:4).

"The pride of man shall be brought low" (Isa. 2:17, A.S.V.).

"God resisteth the proud" (Jas. 4:6).

No further words are necessary to express the hatred, the revulsion, the antipathy of God to pride and arrogance, to conceit and haughtiness. It is an abomination to Him. Can we condone what God hates? Can we entertain what is an abomination to Him? God opposes the proud and holds them at a distance. There is no point of meeting between a proud heart and God, but a broken and contrite spirit He will not despise.

THE ESSENCE OF PRIDE

The word "proud" in James 4:6 signifies literally "one who considers himself above other people." It is an offense to both God and man. The Greeks hated it. Theophylact called pride "the citadel and summit of all evils."

Pride is a *deification of self*. It thinks more highly of itself than it ought to think. It arrogates to itself the honor which belongs to God only. It caused Rabbi Simeon Ben Jochai to say with becoming humility, "If there are only two righteous men in the world, I and my son are the two. If only one, I am he." It was the sin of Nebuchadnezzar which brought him down to the level of the beasts. The valet of the last German Kaiser said, "I cannot deny that my master was vain. He had to be the central figure in everything. If he went to a christening, he wanted to be the baby. If he went to a wedding, he wanted to be the bride. If he went to a funeral, he wanted to be the corpse."

Pride is characterized by *independence of God*. It was at the heart of Adam's sin. Instead of being dependent on God, he desired to be as God and brought ruin on the whole race. Pride desires to be beholden to neither God nor man. It is perfectly self-sufficient, in striking contrast to the Son of God who said, "I can of mine own self do nothing" (John 5:30). He gloried in His dependence on His Father. Pride glories in being self-made.

It involves a certain *contempt for others*. "God, I thank thee, that I am not as other men are . . . or even as this publican" (Luke 18:11). It relegates every other mortal to a minor role in life. It uses other people as a backdrop to display its own brilliance. The proud man considers others beneath him, the *hoi polloi*, the common herd. Instead of pouring contempt on all his pride, he pours his contempt on others whom he esteems less worthy than himself.

Pride is *essentially competitive* in its nature. C. S. Lewis points out that no one is proud because he is rich, or clever, or good-looking. He is proud because he is richer, or more clever, or better-looking than someone else. It involves a comparison which always goes in favor of the one who makes it.

THE MANIFESTATION OF PRIDE

Pride adapts itself to every temperament, accommodates itself to every situation. It is remarkably fluid. It can be humble or haughty at will. There is a form suited to every character. We do well to ask ourselves what are our particular forms of pride. Of face, race, place, grace? Of intellect, achievement, success, skill?

There is *intellectual pride*, for "knowledge puffeth up." This was the peculiar temptation of the brilliant Corinthians who prided themselves on their mental superiority. Seven of the eight passages in which "puffed up" is used occur in the Corinthian epistles. This form of pride tends to manifest itself in scornful superiority over those of limited intellectual gift, or who have been denied opportunity of advanced education. It flourishes luxuriantly in the student to whom a new world of knowledge is opening and who has not yet learned that *true* learning begets humility, not conceit. It was different with Charles Dickens. People who met him for the first time would never have suspected that he was the most distinguished literary man of his time.

In the East we are reaping the harvest we have sown in our *racial pride* which despises those of a different color of skin or culture. Those who cherish this hateful attitude have not yet learned that differences of race and culture do not necessarily involve inferiority in any respect. Indeed, the longer contact we have with people of other races, the less foundation we discover for our vaunted superiority.

There is a *social pride* which preens itself on an accident of birth for which it can take no credit. It despises the common herd who do not move in such select circles of society. The lesson that nobility of character is not the exclusive possession of any one class or group has yet to be mastered.

Charles Lamb once accosted one of these grandiose people
with the remark, "Excuse me, sir, but are you—anybody in
particular?"

But more abhorrent to God than any of these is *spiritual
pride,* pride of grace. It is very possible to be proud of the
spiritual gifts God has entrusted to us and to strut about
ostentatiously, forgetting that we have nothing which we
have not received, that grace is a gift, an undeserved favor.
We can actually be filled with pride at the eloquence and
brilliance of our sermon on humility. But the most perfect
lens is that which allows us to forget the glass is there at all.
Dr. John McNeill told of a lady who approached him at the
close of a sermon on humility. "Yes, Dr. McNeill," she vol-
unteered, "humility is my forte!"

Pride manifests itself in the inordinate assertion of self.
The man in the grip of pride worships at the shrine of self.
Like Narcissus gazing into the fountain, he is infatuated with
himself. Seeing the image of his own beauty, Narcissus took
it for a water nymph and fell in love with it. So infatuated
was he that when he could not obtain the object of his
passion, he committed suicide. He was the perfect example
of the folly of being a lover of oneself.

The unbroken, proud man thirsts for and eagerly drinks in
flattery and praise because it gratifies his self-love. He is
elated when it is given, depressed when it is withheld. There
is no one in the world about whom he delights to talk more
than about himself. He will turn every conversation until
it centers on himself. In the palace of Wurtzung there is a
hall of glass known as the Hall of a Thousand Mirrors. You
enter—a thousand hands are stretched out to greet you. You
smile, and a thousand smiles greet your smile; you weep,
and a thousand eyes weep with you. But they are all your
own hands and smiles and tears. Such is the proud man, en-
grossed in himself, surrounded by self, imprisoned by self.
The Master stands out in striking contrast to all such. In the
delicate task of announcing His Messiahship to His own
townspeople, He accomplished it without the use of the pro-

noun "I." Reading Isaiah 61:1 and 2 He said, "This day is this Scripture fulfilled in your ears." The only One whose prerogative it is to say "I," in His humility avoided its use.

Pride defiles everything it touches. There are germs which transform nourishing food into virulent poison. Pride transforms virtues into vices and blessings into curses. Beauty plus pride results in vanity. Zeal plus pride makes for tyranny and cruelty. Human wisdom compounded with pride brings infidelity. In speech, pride manifests itself in criticism, for criticism is always made from the vantage point of conscious superiority. Pride will find cause for criticism in everyone and everything. It lauds itself and belittles its neighbor.

Scripture is replete with illustrations of the folly and tragedy which follow in the train of pride. It was pride of his kingdom and power that moved king David to number Israel, a sin which resulted in Divine judgment (I Chron. 21:1). Gripped by pride, Hezekiah showed his covetous enemies "all the house of his precious things, the silver, and the gold . . . and all that was found in his treasures" (II Kings 20:13)—and lost them all. Nebuchadnezzar's pride fed on his own achievements. "Is not this great Babylon that I have built for the house of the kingdom by the might of my power and for the honor of my majesty?" But his haughty spirit went before a gigantic fall. "While the word was in the king's mouth there fell a voice from heaven, saying, The kingdom is departed from thee, and they shall drive thee from men, and thy dwelling shall be with the beasts of the field: they shall make thee to eat grass as oxen." When his sanity was restored, the center of his worship was shifted from himself to God. "Now I Nebuchadnezzar praise and extol and honor the King of heaven" (Dan. 4:37). Pride is a species of moral and spiritual insanity.

Uzziah's heart was lifted up in pride by his supposed military might and success. "But when he was strong, his heart was lifted up to his destruction: for he transgressed against the Lord his God, and went into the temple of the Lord to burn incense upon the altar of incense and . . . leprosy even rose up in his forehead" (II Chron. 26:16, 19). Pride led him to intrude on the Divine prerogatives and when he died, they said, "He is a leper." Herod lapped up the praise the people of Tyre accorded to his oration, "It is the voice of a god, and not of a man. And immediately the angel of the Lord smote him, because he gave not God the glory" (Acts 12:22, 23). Peter's pride made him feel so superior in moral courage to his fellow-disciples that he boasted, "Though all men forsake thee, yet will not I." It was not long before his boasting pride suffered a shattering blow when he "denied him with oaths and curses." ·

THE PROOF OF PRIDE

The subtlety of pride is seen in the fact that its victims are generally quite oblivious to their bondage, though all around can hear the clank of the chains. On one occasion a man said to his friend, "Well, I can thank God that whatever my other faults are, I am not proud." "I can well understand that," rejoined the other, "for of course you haven't very much to be proud about." "Haven't I, indeed?" was the indignant rejoinder. "I've got as much to be proud about as you have!" If we are honest with ourselves, it will not be difficult to discover the extent to which pride rules in our lives. There are infallible tests by which we can discover its hateful presence.

The Test of Precedence. How do we react when another is selected for the office we coveted? When another is promoted, while we are overlooked? When another is honored and we are ignored? When another outshines us? Does it stimulate jealousy and ill-will or can we really rejoice in another's advancement or greater ability? Do we, like Diotrephes, love to have the foremost place? It is true that the most difficult instrument in the orchestra to master is sec-

ond fiddle. It was this test that came to John the Baptist
when the crowds left him to follow Jesus, but he passed it
with triumph. "He must increase, but I must decrease."
"This my joy is fulfilled."

The Test of Sincerity. We will say all kinds of bad things
about ourselves, but how do we feel when others say these
same things of us? Many of our self-depreciatory statements
are insincere and we realize them to be so when others
affirm the same of us. Many a man declines office only that
he might be pressed a little harder.

The Test of Criticism. What is our reaction to criticism?
Do we immediately fly to justify ourselves? Does it arouse
hostility and resentment in us? Do we immediately begin
to criticize our critic? Such responses to criticism are the
surest proof that we are in the grip of pride. We cannot
bear to have people speak of us except with approbation.
Humility will take criticism no matter from whom it comes,
and will profit by it because it knows that where there is
smoke there is fire, and there is usually some element of
truth from which it can profit in the most scathing criticism.

The Test of Inferiority. People with an inferiority complex are not necessarily free from pride. Indeed that very
complex may be the clear index of a pride which is hurt because others do not accept them at their own valuation. It
may be pride of a different kind but pride nonetheless. Our
pride is hurt because we think people consider us inferior,
whereas in our own heart of hearts, no matter how much we
protest to the contrary, we do not feel as inferior as they
appear to think.

THE CURE OF PRIDE

Pride must be radically dealt with. William Law wrote,
"Pride must die in you or nothing of heaven can live in you.
. . . Look not at pride only as an unbecoming temper, nor at
humility only as a decent virtue. . . . One is all hell and the
other all heaven."

Steps on the road to cure are:

Perception. Humility, the antithesis of pride, has been defined by Bernard as the virtue by which man becomes conscious of his own unworthiness. We will never conquer a sin of which we are unconscious or over which we do not grieve. We must hate what God hates. Self-knowledge is not easy to come by, as we are all so prepossessed in our own favor. We see the splinter in our brother's eye with great clarity but, with strange inconsistency, fail to detect the plank in our own. We need to genuinely ask God to expose us to ourselves. When we see ourselves as we truly are, we will sink in self-abasement. Is it not true that we would not be very comfortable if others knew all our secret thoughts, saw all the pictures that hang on the walls of our imagination, perceived all our hidden motives, observed all our covered deeds, heard all our whispered words? Are we humbled that God knows us for the persons we truly are? If we realize the facts about ourselves as they really are, all grounds for pride will be demolished. Do I know a lot? What I know is infinitesimal compared with what remains to be known. Am I clever? My cleverness is a gift for which I can take no credit. Am I rich? It was God who gave me the power to get wealth.

Chastening. As a preventive against loathsome pride in His children, God lovingly disciplines them. Paul had this experience. "And lest I should be exalted above measure through the abundance of the revelations, there was given to me a thorn in the flesh . . . lest I should be exalted above measure" (II Cor. 12:7). Do we recognize, in some crippling limitation, some painful malady, some thwarted ambition, the gracious ministry of God to deliver us from something worse, the ascendancy of pride?

Mortification. A prudent farmer cuts down weeds when they are young lest they spread their seeds and multiply. So let us observe the proud thought, confess it and put it away. Cherish the proud thought and you will find you have

nursed a viper in your bosom. Pride is of the flesh and the
Spirit will help us in this activity. "If you *through the Spirit*
do mortify the deeds of the body, ye shall live" (Rom. 8:13).

Comparison. We compare ourselves among ourselves and
come off fairly well in the comparison. But let us compare
ourselves with the perfect Christ and if we are honest we
will be overwhelmed with the tawdriness and shabbiness
or even the vileness of our characters. While the disciples
in their pride wrangled to secure first place, the Lord of
glory donned the slave's smock and washed their dirty feet.
It is striking that Satan tempted Christ with the very sin
which had caused his own downfall, but where he suc-
cumbed, Christ triumphed.

Contemplation. The final secret is the contemplation of
Christ. Our best efforts of self-discovery and self-discipline
will be inadequate alone to root out this cancer. It requires
a radical and supernatural change of heart, and this is what
is promised. "Beholding . . . the glory of the Lord, we are
being changed into the same image" (II Cor. 3:18). Pride
shrivels and withers and shrinks away in the light of His
humility. And again it is "by the Spirit of the Lord" that the
transformation takes place. The Holy Spirit will always
cooperate to the limit with anyone who comes to hate his
pride and covets the humility of Christ.

THE SATISFYING COMPENSATIONS
OF GOD

*"Lo, I see four men . . . and the form of the fourth is
like the Son of God"* (Dan. 3:25)

READING: Daniel 3:1-30

IN THE DAYS of our childhood this story seemed very remote
and, while we may not have doubted its veracity, it appeared to be quite without relevance to the times in which
we lived. But only a few months ago a missionary of the
China Inland Mission who had just returned from a visit
to Burma, told a comparable story of Titus, a former student of his in China. When he would not deny his faith,
Communist officials in southwest China held him over a fire;
then urged him to recant, but without success. The ghastly
process was repeated until the chariot of fire carried him
into the presence of his Lord, charred in body but dauntless
in faith. So this story is right up to date, very relevant to
those who even today may stand in Titus' place.

Picture the exact circumstances these three young men
faced. Impressed by their caliber, Nebuchadnezzar had
shown them favor, much to the displeasure of the Babylonian courtiers. Their jealousy was understandable. Do we
relish seeing foreigners given privileged positions in our
country? Are we without our own national jealousy? The
courtiers determined that in some way they would remove
these three interlopers. The edict that all must worship
Nebuchadnezzar's golden image, erected to celebrate his
victories and enhance his glory, provided a welcome opportunity.

The three young men were in no doubt of the course they should adopt. Had Jehovah not commanded, "Thou shalt not make any graven image" and "Thou shalt have no other gods before me"? When they refused to bow to his image, "then was Nebuchadnezzar full of fury" (v. 19). If they would not bend to his will, they would burn in his furnace. "Heat the furnace seven times hotter than usual," he raged. Such is the background of the story.

THE RESOURCES OF FAITH

The magnificence of their faith is seen in their unwavering refusal to be disloyal to their God, with a seven-times heated furnace as the only alternative. Theirs was dauntless faith indeed. It was expressed in these sublime words, "O Nebuchadnezzar, we are not careful to answer thee in this matter. If it be so, our God whom we serve is able to deliver us from the burning fiery furnace, and he will deliver us out of thine hand, O king. But if not, be it known unto thee, O king, that we will not serve thy gods, nor worship the golden image which thou hast set up" (Dan. 3: 17-18).

Note the resources of faith in their confession.

Faith in the ability of God to deliver them was their first resource. "Our God is able to deliver us." We all subscribe to the ability of God to do everything in general, but it takes the exercise of faith to believe that God is able to do the something in particular which is our concern—especially if we already feel the heat of the fiery furnace! Could anything have seemed more impossible than deliverance? Is my God able to deliver me in my particular furnace of trial? Am I willing to step out in faith and trust Him?

Confidence in the willingness of God to deliver them. "And He will deliver us out of thine hand." This is the second resource of faith. Many who concede the ability of God to do everything are not so confident of His willingness to intervene in their case. To know God is to be assured of His

absolute willingness to intervene in the way He sees to be
in our highest interests. The Lord did deliver the three men,
but in a way they never envisaged. Indeed, at first it seemed
that they were not to be delivered at all.

> Thrice blest is he to whom is given
> The wisdom that can tell
> That God is on the field when He
> Is most invisible.

When the leper appealed to Jesus for healing, he said,
"Lord, if thou wilt, thou canst make me clean"—confident
of His ability, but uncertain of His willingness, Jesus immediately corrected his mistaken concept with the words,
"*I will;* be thou clean."

But the faith of these young men was not at an end with
this second resource. Enshrined in the words "but if not,"
they had a third resource which rendered them invincible
and fireproof.

Acceptance of the sovereignty of God. "But if not, be it
known unto thee, O king . . . we will not worship the golden
image." If we have this third resource of faith, if we can
master this lesson, we are on the road to spiritual maturity.
Even if God had not delivered them, their faith would not
have been staggered. They knew it would be because He
had some better thing for them. They recognized that it
might not be God's purpose to exercise His ability in this
way and were content to leave the issue in His hands. They
understood the principle Jesus stated in parable, "Cannot
I do what I will with mine own?"

Their attitude was, "Even if God does not do as we expect,
our faith will not be stumbled, our confidence in Him and
His love will remain unshaken. We know our God so well
that we are prepared to accept His sovereign will even if
we cannot understand it." In the event itself, there was
apparent cause for their faith to be stumbled, for their cou-
rageous loyalty was rewarded by their being cast into the
furnace after all. The onlooker might be justified in con-

cluding that God was unconcerned, but their faith rose even
to this test. To them, loyalty to their God was more important than life itself. They trusted Him where they could
not trace His purposes. And God rewarded them on the
scale of their magnificent trust. He had secret plans of
grace and blessing of which they had never dreamed.

THE IMPLICATIONS OF FAITH

Thomas Carlyle once said, "The final question which each
of us is compelled to answer is, 'Wilt thou be a hero or a
coward?' " This question constantly confronts us in one form
or another. *Faith is always confronted with a choice.* We
can choose either the high road or the low road. The choice
for these young men was no easy one, nor will it be for us.
Often it is an agonizing experience. Think of choosing between worshiping the king's image or being incinerated in
the king's inferno! Nebuchadnezzar did not demand that
they deny their faith, only that they bow to his image. In
the days of the early church, the mere offering of a pinch
of incense to the emperor would have spared many a martyr
from being thrown to the lions. Faith always chooses the
highest and best even although it be the most costly.

Faith always involves a risk. If there is no risk involved,
no faith is necessary. If we can see the path ahead, we are
walking by sight. What constituted Abraham the father
of the faithful? The key to his whole life of faith is seen
at its beginning. "Abraham went out, *not knowing whither*
he went." He was willing to risk all on God. We exercise
faith only when the way ahead is not clear, when we are
so placed that we have no alternative if God lets us down.
Not everyone enjoys taking such risks. Many who are bold
as lions in taking physical risks are strangely timorous when
it comes to taking a step of faith. We like to play safe, to
have our plans cut and dried, to have an alternative ready.
There is always a risk in the pathway of faith.

Faith always encounters opposition. The pathway of faith is not primrose-strewn, it is blood-marked. Abraham advanced from one test to another, each more difficult than the last. There was always opposition to be overcome, difficulty to be overleaped. Instead of repining at the difficulties we meet we should rejoice at the fresh opportunity they afford for the exercise of faith. If we are advancing in the walk of faith, we can expect to encounter more opposition, inward and outward, than our fellows. How else could faith have its exercise? There would be no incentive to climb.

THE DELIVERANCE OF FAITH

There are two important lessons to master.

Deliverance from trial is not necessarily our highest good. God did not deliver the three men *from* the fiery furnace but He did deliver them *in* it. We must get away from the idea that deliverance from trial is the highest form of spiritual blessing. That is an attitude which is entirely alien to the spirit of the New Testament. Was it the attitude of the Lord whom we follow? Paul gloried in enduring tribulation, not in evading it. God could easily have prevented the three young men from being flung into the furnace. He had something much better for them. There has been too much emphasis in Second Advent teaching on escape from the tribulation which is to overtake this old world. Without engaging in any millennial controversy, we should be alive to an emphasis which is unwholesome. Our Lord categorically stated, "In the world ye shall have tribulation," and it is the complacent church which knows little tribulation which makes little spiritual impact. God nowhere promises us immunity from trial. We learn more in a few days in the fiery furnace than we would learn in years out of it. We emerge from the trials with a greater God.

The incidence of trial is unequal. God does not treat all alike. This obvious fact causes some to be offended in God. These three young men were not concerned with God's treatment of others. They had their dealings direct with Him. We quickly run into spiritual trouble if we look around at God's dealings with others. Our Lord taught Peter a salutary lesson on this point. He was concerned lest John should receive preferential treatment. Jesus replied sternly, "What is that to thee? Follow thou me." James went from prison to the executioner's block. Peter went from prison to a prayer meeting. Peter won 3,000 souls. Stephen received 3,000 stones. We have to accept the fact that "the ways of the Lord are not equal." He does not deal with us on the mass-production principle. He delivers some from trial. He delivers some in trial.

Do we have a "But if not" in our spiritual vocabulary? Do we have this third resource of faith? Is our faith fireproof? If wars should arise and son, daughter, husband, sweetheart be taken from our side, have we a "But if not" to carry us through that fiery furnace? If business should fail, or financial reverses be experienced? If ill-health grips us? When old age enfeebles us? When bereavement strikes? When desire for a life partner is not granted? When cherished plans are thwarted? If Christian work does not meet with the success we envisaged? When we are not designated to the mission station we expected or to live with the fellow-worker we would choose? Let us emulate the dauntless faith of the noble three who maintained their confidence in God in the face of seemingly unrewarded faith. "But if not, we will still go on trusting God," said the three men. They did not fall into self-pity or unbelief.

We may not always understand God's dealings with us at the time, and He nowhere undertakes to explain Himself. "What I do thou knowest not now, but thou shalt know hereafter," is His promise. In the meantime we learn many a lesson in the furnace of testing.

If all my days were summer, how could I know
What my Lord means by His, "whiter than the snow"?
If all my days were sunny, could I say
In His fair land He wipes all tears away?

If I were never weary, could I keep
Close to my heart, "He gives His loved ones sleep"?
    Were no graves mine, might I not come to deem
    The life eternal but a baseless dream?

My winter and my tears and weariness,
Even my graves may be His way to bless.
    I call them ills, yet that can surely be
    Nothing but love that shows my Lord to me.

THE COMPENSATIONS OF FAITH

Their faith did not go unappreciated or unrewarded.

Companionship with the Son of God was their first joyous privilege. "Lo, I see four men loose, walking in the midst of the fire, and they have no hurt; and the form of the fourth is like the Son of God" (v. 25). In the furnace of affliction the Lord draws nearer than at any other time. It was not until they were "in the midst of the fire" that the Lord joined them. They acted in faith and He responded after they had risked all on Him.

Control of the flames was another compensation. God saw that the flames burned with a strange discrimination. "And the princes . . . saw these men, upon whose bodies the fire had no power, nor was a hair of their head singed, neither were their coats changed, nor the smell of fire had passed upon them" (v. 27). The flames burnt only their bonds, enabling them to walk in fellowship with the Son of God in unfettered freedom. Can we not see in this one of the gracious compensations of the fires of testing?

Vindication of their own faith and of their God was one of the rewards of their unwavering confidence. Why the details about their bodies, and hair, and coats? And why no smell of fire? An anonymous writer says: "High in rank and honor was the Babylonian god Izbar, the god of fire. Before the eyes of king and prince, governor, captains and counselors, this god must be defeated. The king had challenged the defeat by his own action. And now the defeat is overwhelming. On their own ground Jehovah has met these ardent believers in the god of fire, and they find that He is present, not merely as a tribal god in Palestine, but as the God of Heaven and earth in Babylon also, as able and willing to deliver only three of His children as to help thirty thousand if need were. Let us suppose for a moment that the three men had come out with the marks of fire partially upon them, or even with the smell of it, that here and there the fire had singed either body or garment, and what would have been the attitude of the fire-worshipers? Something like this, 'Ah, well, it is true Izbar has not been able to destroy them, but he has at least left his mark upon them. They will wear these clothes no more. Their friends will scarcely recognize them as the men they once were. The smell of the furnace will not soon leave them. They have not come out scatheless. Our Izbar is still a god to be reckoned with. They will not be so ready to disobey the king's mandate another time. They will not come out of the furnace, it may be, a second time as easily as they have done this time.'

"And so the whole moral effect of the protest of these three Hebrews would have been discounted. The dexterity of the world in evading direct issues of this kind is marvelous. But in this case evasion was impossible. Not one loophole of escape was left them. In awe they had to admit that Jehovah had conquered, that the miracle was perfect and unquestionable, and that 'the smell of fire had not passed on' the three brave followers of the Most High."

There is many another similar illustration of an undaunted faith which had its "But if not" in the face of devastating alternatives. Each demonstrates a faith that is not only obedient to the Divine commands but triumphs over the Divine contradictions.

Job lost all—home, herd, family, health, even his wife's sympathy—yet in the midst of the holocaust his faith triumphed gloriously. "He shall bring me forth to the light, and I shall behold Him." *But if not*, "though he slay me, yet will I trust him." Job had the third resource of faith.

Imagine the poignancy of Isaac's question to Abraham, "Where is the lamb for the burnt offering?" Abraham had his answer ready. "God will provide a lamb," *but if not*, I will still trust, accounting that God is "able to raise him up even from the dead" (Heb. 11:19). Such a thing as a resurrection had never been dreamed of, but Abraham's faith rose to the occasion and he received him back from the dead in a figure.

John the Baptist was languishing in prison. He was disappointed that he had received no message from Jesus, that He had taken no steps to liberate, or even visit him. He sent his disciples with the question, "Master, am I mistaken? Art Thou He that should come, or look we for another? *But if not*, my faith is not stumbled. I will keep on looking for another."

The Lord Jesus was agonizing in prayer in Gethsemane, in such distress that bloody sweat forced its way through his pores. "Father, if it be possible, let this cup pass from Me. *But if not*, Thy will be done."

Can we wonder that Nebuchadnezzar was impotent against such a faith as this? The fire had no power over the bodies of the dauntless trio and he had no power over their spirits. The world is powerless to lure or daunt men with a faith such as this. The Devil is powerless to do more than burn their bonds and send them forth as God's free men.

In the world of today the testing flames may very well lick around us too. There is always an image somewhere demanding our worship. The form of the furnace may change with the years but not the fact. The world may threaten to cast us into the furnace of social ostracism. If we do not bow to the god of popular custom we will be fed to the flames of ridicule and popularity. It is not inconceivable that actual fires of persecution may rage around us yet. It is for us to be certain that we possess the fireproof faith of the three young men if we are to enjoy the abundant compensations of God.

PART II

THE SUPREME VISION OF CHRIST

"I saw one like unto the Son of man" (Rev. 1:12, 13)

READING: Revelation 1:9-20

THE SYMBOLIC MESSAGE of the Book of the Revelation of Jesus Christ has ever been treasured most by a church passing through the fires of testing and persecution. For this reason it has special relevance for large segments of the world of today. Throughout history the self-revelation of God has always been appropriate to the contemporary needs of His people, and of no portion of Scripture is this more true than of the Apocalypse. To the exiled John is entrusted the privileged task of unveiling Christ in a character exactly suited to the needs of a harassed and persecuted church.

Such a message demands a sympathetic messenger and, that he might be thus prepared, God permitted John to be banished to Patmos where, according to Victorinus, along with a gang of criminals he had to work in the mines of that rocky island. It was on account of his loyalty to the Word of God and his testimony to Jesus Christ that he was in exile. Indeed, early Christian tradition maintained that he was under sentence for failure to yield to the demands of emperor-worship. From the vantage point of his identification with his Asian fellow-believers in their tribulation, he was qualified to bring them the Divine message. He sat where they sat.

Of this particular Lord's Day, for by the second century this phrase had become the technical title for Sunday, John wrote that he "came to be in the Spirit," that state of ecstasy and elevated consciousness in which the prophet sees visions and hears words beyond his normal capacity to understand. It was as though he had been transported from the world of time and space into eternity. Paul had a similar experience. He was transported to "the third heaven" and heard "unspeakable words, which it is not lawful for man to utter" (II Cor. 12:4). So entirely possessed and controlled by the Spirit was John that the outward world receded and the invisible world became tangible and real.

While in this ecstatic state John heard behind him "a great voice as of a trumpet" with its insistent, commanding clarity. It was the sound of a trumpet which summoned God's ancient people to their religious feasts. It was a trumpet-voice which accompanied God's revelation of Himself at Sinai (Exod. 19:6; 20:18). It is not surprising that to one whose mind was steeped and saturated in the Old Testament Scriptures, the visions of the Apocalypse were communicated to him through Old Testament symbolism and imagery.

HIS UNIQUE PERSON

When John turned to see the speaker, he saw none other than the Living Christ—"one like unto a Son of Man"—whom he had last seen sixty years previously. No longer is He "despised and rejected of men, a man of sorrows and acquainted with grief," but the transcendent triumphant Christ, clothed in inconceivable majesty and glory, standing in the midst of the seven golden lampstands which symbolized the seven churches of Asia. It was the very same Jesus on whose breast John had often laid his head, and yet how strikingly different from the days of His humiliation. The same, yet not the same; possessing the same human attributes, yet vested with awful power and majesty.

The vision was spiritual and the description symbolical, yet it presents to the mind a picture of Christ more vivid and impressive than any painting. It is not for us to endeavor from the imagery here used to conjure up a grotesque literal

picture of the One whom John saw, but rather to interpret
the symbols in which the inspired vision was given in the
light of their use elsewhere in Scripture. Through the significance of the symbolism we can discover the meaning
of the vision. Artists of all ages have endeavored to repro-
duce on canvas the face and form of Christ, but it is a remarkable fact that the Gospels contain not a line concerning His physical appearance, striking though that must have
been. The only picture we have of Him is in the inspired
words which present to us His moral and spiritual characteristics.

The first thing to impress John in the vision was *the clothing* of Christ. He was "clothed with a garment down to the
foot and girt about the breasts with a golden girdle" (v. 13),
a long flowing robe with a golden belt buckled at the breast.
It was a garment fitted for dignified and majestic movement,
the repose of sovereignty. It contrasted with the workaday
robe which was girded at the loins, fitted for speedy service.

His function was suggested by His clothing. It was the
robe characteristic of prophets, priests, and kings, and therefore eminently suited to the One in whom all three offices
found their climax and fulfillment. It was the robe of the
prophet, the bearer of the inspired message of God (Dan.
10:5). It was the garment worn by the high priest when en-
gaged in his duty of trimming and supervising the shining
of the lamps in the sanctuary. It was the robe of royalty
(I Sam. 18:24). Thus the One whom John saw is competent
to impart the Divine message to man, to introduce him into
the holiest of all, and to reign over him in righteousness.
There were no doubts in John's mind of the Deity of this
august Personage, for he ascribed to Him titles which in the
Old Testament are used exclusively of God.

A full-length portrait of the exalted Lord follows, a sevenfold representation which in vivid colors and by graphic
metaphor throws into bold relief His moral and spiritual
attributes and His judicial powers.

"*His head and his hairs* were white like wool, as white as

snow" (v. 14). The symbolism is drawn from Daniel. "I beheld till the thrones were cast down, and the Ancient of Days did sit, whose garment was white as snow, and the hair of his head like the pure wool" (Dan. 7:9). Here is the evident combination of antiquity and purity, of pre-existence and sinlessness. His is the great age and wisdom of eternity. "His is the age that is not aged, and the purity and holiness which are eternal." The raiment of the Ancient of Days glistened like snow in sunshine. When John saw the Son of Man on Mount Tabor, "his raiment was white and glistering" (Luke 9:29), "shining, exceeding white as snow; so as no fuller on earth can white them" (Mark 9:3). Here is *holiness perfect and mature.*

"*His eyes* were as a flame of fire" (v. 14), symbol of that penetrating vision and infinite knowledge which is peculiar to omniscience. In Daniel's vision, His "eyes were as flaming torches" (10:6). This vivid symbol indicates His power to scrutinize and search every life, to penetrate the inner chambers of every imagination, to "bring to light the hidden things of darkness and make manifest the counsels of the heart." It appears again in Revelation 19:11, 12. "And I saw heaven opened, and behold a white horse; and he that sat upon him was called Faithful and True, and in righteousness he doth judge and make war. His eyes were as a flame of fire, and on his head were many crowns." Here the emphasis is upon His consuming indignation as Executor of the righteous judgment of God against sin, "in flaming fire taking vengeance on them that know not God, and that obey not the gospel of our Lord Jesus Christ" (II Thess. 1:8). But Christ's judgment, unlike ours, is based on perfect knowledge. "I know thy works" is His reiterated assurance to each of the seven churches, and His assurance that every credit will be given. Nothing, whether favorable or adverse, can be concealed from the eyes of Him who possesses *perfect knowledge.*

"*His feet* like unto fine brass, as if they burned in a furnace" (v. 15). The symbolism here is not easy to interpret.

The figure reappears in Revelation 2:18 and is followed by Christ's activity in judgment (vv. 23, 27). Christ walks among the churches and moves toward the consummation of God's eternal purpose. Brass in John's day was a compound of gold, copper, and silver, the strongest metal known. Here it is brass which has reached white heat in a furnace. One characteristic of brass was that it would not yield to heat. Christ, as man, could stand the furnace of God's holiness. Though walking in a world defiled by sin, He contracted no taint or corruption. But the figure could also suggest His inflexible and invincible procedure in judgment when, undeterred and unhindered by the opposition of man or devil, with glowing and flashing feet He treads down all the enemies of righteousness. "He treadeth the winepress of the fierceness and wrath of Almighty God" (Rev. 19:15). It is an awe-inspiring picture of God's irresistible and terrible judgment on rebellious man, and it is the Son of Man whose feet had walked unsullied through the corruption of the world, through whom it is effected. He will execute *perfect judgment.*

"*His voice* as the sound of many waters" (v. 15; Ezek. 43:2). "The voice of His words like the voice of a multitude." What is more impressive than the roar of Niagara in full spate, or a vast crowd in full throat? Such is the voice of Christ, inescapable, authoritative, commanding all men and nations. The same voice that once uttered the sweet invitation, "Come unto me," now resounds like the roar of a mighty cataract. As that loud, reverberating voice fell on John's ear, it was like the mighty waves that pounded Patmos' rocky shores—symbolic of the terribleness of the voice with which He will rebuke and sentence His foes within the church and without. There is a unique finality in the voice of Christ, for no word He spoke ever needed to be recalled. H. B. Swete remarks that the voice of God is not confined to one note. It can be terrible as the surge of the sea, or it can be the voice of gentle stillness, majestic in rebuke or tender in comfort. This is the voice of *perfect authority.*

"He had in His *right hand* seven stars" (v. 16). "The seven stars are the seven angels"—messengers or pastors—"of the seven churches" (v. 20). Christ is represented as holding in His powerful right hand the destiny of the churches. Any authority possessed by these messengers to the churches is derived from Him. He holds and upholds them and they are accountable to Him. He is the Possessor and Upholder of the churches, their Guardian and Sustainer, and the pastors whom He gives to them are secure in His powerful grasp. In the next verse, which records John falling at the feet of the majestic Christ, it is this same right hand which is placed upon his head in reassurance. How safe the messengers to the church are under His *perfect control!*

"Out of *his mouth* went a sharp, two-edged sword" (v. 16). The interpretation of this symbol is found in Hebrews 4:12, A.S.V., "The word of God is living and active and sharper than any two-edged sword . . . quick to discern the thoughts and intents of the heart"—truth piercing, dividing, discerning. The penetrating quality of the Word of Christ, the accuracy of His judgment and diagnosis of the deeds of men is in view, for the words which proceed from His mouth are to be the basis of all future judgment. "The word that I have spoken, the same shall judge him in the last day" (John 12:48). The power of the Word of Christ to reprove and punish is more prominent here than its power to convert, for the sword is the emblem of His judicial authority and power. It cuts into lives, lays bare sin, excises what should not be there and destroys all that is not for the glory of God in the church. In His judgment Christ manifests *perfect discrimination.*

"*His countenance* was as the sun shineth in his strength" (v. 16). The countenance is the sum total of all the features. His entire appearance was like the sun at noon, shining in unclouded strength, too intense for the naked human eye. Was John recalling the vision on the Mount of Transfiguration when "His face did shine as the sun"? The face which John saw now in vision was not "a visage marred more than any man's," but one that blazed with unbearable brightness, leaving an impression of dazzling splendor and awe-full majesty. The pastors are stars. The churches are lamps. Christ is the majestic Sun. Just as the sun is the supreme light-giver to the world, so Christ is the supreme Light-giver to the spiritual world. "And the city had no need of the sun, neither of the moon, to shine in it: for the glory of God did lighten it, and the Lamb is the light thereof" (Rev. 21:23). His countenance mirrors His *perfect moral glory*.

HIS UNIQUE PREROGATIVES

The effect of the vision on John was overwhelming. "When I saw him, I fell at his feet as dead" (v. 17). The vision of God always produces humiliation and prostration. John fell in awed worship and conscious unworthiness before the majesty of Him who is the effulgence of the Father's glory, the exact impress of His person (Heb. 1:3).

Could this majestic, stupendous Personage be the same as the meek and lowly Man on whose breast he had laid his head? Yes, the heart that beats beneath the golden girdle is the same heart. The hands that control the seven stars are the same nail-pierced hands. The eyes that flash fire once wept tears of compassion over doomed Jerusalem. The voice has the same sweet cadences as moved the soldiers to say, "Never man spake like this man." The glowing feet are the very same feet as carried His bleeding body up the slopes of Mount Calvary. The mouth, out of which went the two-edged sword, once framed the invitation, "Come unto me . . . I will give you rest." The radiant countenance is the same as was once "marred more than any man."

But the real purpose of the vision was to encourage and strengthen John, not to terrify him. "He laid his right hand upon me, saying unto me, Fear not; I am the first and the last. . . . I am alive for evermore, Amen; and have the keys of hell and of death" (vv. 17, 18). "I am Alpha and Omega, the beginning and the ending" (v. 8). This compassionate touch and further self-revelation of the Lord was sufficient to raise John to his feet and to reassure him. The nail-pierced hand, strong enough to uphold the universe, was gentle enough to comfort and impart strength to a prostrate, humbled worshiper.

His Unique Assertions

In this vision our Lord made five unique assertions concerning Himself which afforded adequate grounds to dispel John's fears.

"*I am Alpha and Omega*" (vv. 8, 11), an assertion of the eternity of His Godhead. He is the God of all history, its beginning, its end, and the whole course in between, even as between the first and last letters of the Greek alphabet lies every possible form of speech. He is the perfect, complete, and eternal revelation of God. "In Christ, Genesis, the Alpha of the Old Testament, and Revelation, the Omega of the New Testament, meet together: the last book presenting to us man and God reconciled in Paradise, as the first book presented man at the beginning, innocent and in God's favor in Paradise" (Jamieson).

"*I am the beginning and the ending . . . the first and the last*" (vv. 8, 11; cf. Isa. 44:6). All things began with Him and all things will end with Him. He is the origin and goal of all creation. He is first, because before Him there was no God, and last, because after Him there will be no other. He is both Author and Finisher of faith. He is with us at birth; He will be with us at death.

"*I am he that liveth and was dead*" (v. 18), expressing the vivid contrast between the eternal life inherent in Christ and His voluntary surrender to the powers of death. Because He tasted death, He is able to say to death-ridden mankind, "There is no need to fear death. I have trodden that way, exhausted its power, and extracted its sting."

"I am alive for evermore" (v. 18), unto the ages of the ages. Death could not keep its prey. He now lives "in the power of an endless life." Others, like Lazarus, had returned to life only to die again. He rose from the dead and is alive for evermore. His having passed through death as a man and now living in fulness of life is basis for our confidence, since through Him death is but the gateway to fuller life. To a church facing the possibility of martyrdom, this truth was urgently needed to quell fear. "The church could not live if Christ were dead, but because Christ lives, the church cannot die."

"I have the keys of hell and of death" (v. 18), wrested in His resurrection from "him that hath the power of death, the devil." Hades is conceived in Matt. 16:18 as a prison-house or walled city. It is the unseen world to which death is the portal. Keys are the symbol of authority. The keys of the unseen world are in Christ's hand and with them the destiny of all men. We need have no fear of going to any place the keys of which are in His nail-pierced hand. No longer need we fear the grim reaper, the king of terrors. Christ alone admits us to death and opens the way out on the other side. No one can wrest the keys from His control. Because He rose, we shall rise also.

Because this living, majestic, powerful Christ stands in the midst of His churches and holds their destiny in these hands, there is no cause for them or for us to fear.

THE TRANSCENDENT WORTHINESS
OF CHRIST

"Thou art worthy to take the book, and to open the seals thereof: for thou wast slain" (Rev. 5:9)

"Worthy is the Lamb that was slain to receive power, and riches, and wisdom, and strength, and honor, and glory, and blessing" (Rev. 5:12)

READING: Revelation 5:1-14

FOR MORE THAN FORTY YEARS Samuel Chadwick, noted Methodist preacher, commenced each Lord's Day by reading this thrilling chapter. It might well be thought that continual reading would rob the passage of all inspirational power. But not so, and for two reasons. First, because of the inherent vitality of Scripture when illuminated by the Holy Spirit and applied by a sanctified imagination. Second, because in the vision of the ultimate and absolute triumph of Christ over all opposition, he found ever new inspiration for life and service. We, too, can kindle our heart's adoration at the same altar fire and in the strength of that vision fulfill the appointed task.

THE VISION OF THE LAMB

"I beheld, and lo, in the midst of the throne and of the four beasts [living creatures], and in the midst of the elders, stood a Lamb as it had been slain" (v. 6). John the Seer is introduced to a moving and majestic heavenly scene (4:1). A book or scroll, sealed with seven seals, rests in the right hand of Him who is seated on the throne. A mighty angel loudly challenges Heaven and earth and Hell to produce a champion qualified to break open the sealed scroll. In the breathless silence John anxiously scans the assembled myriads for the emergence of his champion. But there is not a stir. No volunteer appears. At last, overcome with dismay, he bursts into uncontrollable weeping because there is no one good enough to look on the scroll, much less to open it.

What is the seven-sealed scroll in which this cosmic crisis centers? Numerous interpretations of its significance have been advanced, for God has more than one book.

Is it *the sealed scroll of Holy Scriptures?* The Old Testament is undoubtedly a closely sealed book unless interpreted in the light of the advent and cross of Christ. To the Jews it is still sealed because they refuse to see Christ in it. How inscrutable are its mysteries without His cross and passion, but how open its message when He is seen on every page!

Is it *the sealed scroll of God's eternal purpose*, His final disposition of the affairs of the universe? The Lamb alone is qualified to interpret and disclose the mind and purpose of God and carry it forward to completion.

Is it *the sealed scroll of the covenant* between God and man which Christ fulfilled in His death, and by right of which He controls the destiny of the world and of the Church?

Is it *the sealed scroll of history*, explaining the past and expounding the future? Apart from Christ, history is without final meaning for real history is the history of redemption. History is His story. John was perplexed to find a satisfying interpretation of the history of his own times with its persecution, trial, and death. What were its meaning and issue? He discovers that the Lamb is the only interpreter of history, the only key to prophecy. He alone can authoritatively tell man where he is going.

De Brugh advances one of the most satisfying suggestions. The sealed scroll is *the title deed to man's inheritance*—an inheritance mortgaged through man's sin but redeemed through the sacrifice of the Lamb. In the scroll are outlined the successive steps by which He will recover it from the usurper and obtain actual possession of the kingdom already purchased for Himself and His elect.

It is significant that the most majestic vision of John's long life came to him when his eyes were wet with tears of conscious unworthiness. His distress was increased by the shattering realization that his disqualification was shared by all creation. "No man was found worthy"—morally fit, sufficiently strong—"to open and to read the book, neither to look thereon" (v. 4). He shared the dilemma of God in dealing with men who are utterly incapable of saving themselves. But God has His own solution for the dilemma.

"Stop weeping," the angel tells John. "Someone is approaching the Throne." But has he the necessary qualifications? He is told that the champion is the Lion of the tribe of Judah. Turning to see the awesome lion he sees—a little lamb encrimsoned with the blood of sacrifice. Christ is announced as the Lion but seen as the Lamb. Redemption is won by self-sacrifice, not by mere might. The Lamb becomes the focus of every eye as He advances to the Throne. Fearlessly He takes the scroll and breaks seal after seal. He alone can redeem man's forfeited inheritance, to which the scroll is the title deed. And His qualifications? Five wounds, mute evidence that He has paid the price of man's lost inheritance and discharged the mortgage.

This is an impressive picture of Christ—still bearing in Heaven the marks of His suffering and death, but evidencing also His Divine prerogatives and attributes. The seven horns symbolize His omnipotence and the seven eyes His omniscience. The seven spirits sent out into all the earth are emblematic of His omnipresence.

As the Lamb takes the now discharged mortgage deed, the assembled hosts burst into a spontaneous and unrestrained song of adoration, swelling to a crescendo in three ascending waves. Ten thousand times ten thousand and thousands of thousands of angels join the four living creatures and the four and twenty elders who raise the tune. The song swells louder and louder until "every creature that is in heaven, and on earth and under the earth, and such as are in the sea and all that are in them"—the universal chorus of creation—is drawn into this exulting paean of praise.

"Thou are worthy to take the book, and to open the seals thereof: for thou wast slain, and hast redeemed us to God by thy blood out of every kindred, and tongue, and people, and nation; and hast made us unto our God kings and priests: and we shall reign on the earth. . . .

"Worthy is the Lamb that was slain to receive power, and riches, and wisdom, and strength, and honor, and glory and blessing. . . . Blessing and honor, and glory, and power, be unto him that sitteth upon the throne, and unto the Lamb for ever and ever" (Rev. 5:9, 10, 12, 13).

"The final vision of the universe," writes William Barclay, "is a universe praising Christ; and it is our privilege to lend our voices and our lives to this vast chorus of praise, for that chorus is necessarily incomplete so long as there is one voice missing from it."

THE ASCRIPTION OF WORTHINESS

We are by nature essentially selfish beings. And even after we have been made partakers of the Divine nature, so strong is the power of the old life that we are usually more interested in receiving than in giving. Was not our Lord's ninth beatitude, "It is more blessed to give than to receive," a tacit correction of this tendency? In our relationship with God we are constantly at the receiving end. We commence our Christian life by receiving the atonement (Rom. 5:11). We continue our Christian life by receiving the abundance of grace (Rom. 5:17). We conclude our Christian life by being received into glory (I Tim. 3:16). We are constantly tugging at God's skirts for some desired blessing, and He delights to have it so, but we forget that He too yearns to receive from us what we alone can give Him.

In one sense we cannot enrich Christ. But nothing is more gladdening to Him than the spontaneous voicing of our appreciation of His intrinsic worth, and nothing is more enriching to ourselves, for "it is in the process of being worshiped that God communicates His presence to men." Writing in this connection, C. S. Lewis says, "To see what the doctrine really means, we must suppose ourselves to be in perfect love with God—drunk with, drowned in, dissolved by that delight which, far from remaining pent up within ourselves as incommunicable, hence hardly tolerable bliss, flows out from us incessantly again in effortless and perfect expression, our joy no more separable from the praise in which it liberates and utters itself than the brightness of a mirror is separable from the brightness it sheds. The Scottish catechism says that man's chief end is 'to glorify God and to enjoy Him forever.' But we shall then know that these are the same thing. Fully to enjoy is to glorify. In commanding us to glorify Him, God is inviting us to enjoy Him."

The perspective of eternity apparently corrects the outlook of the saints, for the universal throng sings with one voice, "Worthy is the Lamb *to receive* . . ." Then follows a sevenfold ascription of worthiness. These seven qualities are grouped under the single Greek article, as though to sum up in one glorious word all that can be given to the Lamb by men and angels.

THE HEPTAD OF PRAISE

The Lamb is worthy to receive:

Power. The French nation deemed Napoleon worthy to receive unlimited power. The German nation entrusted Hitler with unrestricted power. They discovered too late that their confidence was sadly misplaced. To their cost they proved the truth of Lord Acton's assertion: "All power corrupts. Absolute power corrupts absolutely." These men were unworthy either to receive power or to exercise it. Only He who is all merciful is worthy to receive absolute power. The indelible marks of His passion and death are the guarantee that in His hands power will never be abused. It will never degenerate into tyranny or despotism. The sceptor of universal sovereignty is held in a nail-pierced hand. The Lamb is worthy to receive power.

Riches. Although appointed heir of all things, Christ certainly did not receive riches during His earthly life. On the contrary, at times He had not where to lay His head. He often depended on the women of his entourage for support. So poor was He that at His death His total personal estate consisted of the single garment left Him by the gambling soldiers. Small wonder Paul used His voluntary impoverishment to stimulate Corinthian liberality. "Ye know the grace of our Lord Jesus Christ," he exhorted, "that though he was rich, yet for your sakes he became poor, that ye through his poverty might be rich." True riches are moral and spiritual, not financial. "Love is the gold of glory." The unloved rich man is tragically poverty-stricken. Our Lord's becoming poor consisted in His leaving the harmony of Heaven for the discord of earth, the adoration of angels for the malignity of men. The Lamb has earned the right to receive and enjoy the true riches.

Wisdom. Not every learned man is a wise man. Wisdom is more than erudition. It is the ability to make the right use of knowledge. In his youth Solomon prayed for wisdom and his prayer was answered. When the queen of Sheba had seen all Solomon's wisdom, she said to the king, "Behold, the half was not told me: thy wisdom and prosperity exceedeth the fame of which I heard" (I Kings 10:7). Using the background of this very incident Christ said of Himself, "Behold, a greater than Solomon is here" (Matt. 12:42). Christ is the wisdom of God, the source and fount of all true wisdom (I Cor. 1:24). His infinite knowledge is always used for the highest and most beneficent ends. In his humiliation the wise men brought Him their gifts. In His exaltation the highest wisdom given is expressed in placing upon His head the crown of wisdom. The Lamb is worthy to receive wisdom.

Strength. There is a difference between physical and moral strength. Samson had physical strength but not moral strength. Physically powerful, he was morally and spiritually weak. Moral strength is the highest strength. The strength of the Lamb is full-orbed. He is the Strong Man who overcame the devil and spoiled his goods (Luke 11:22). There was no personal situation with which He did not cope. He manifested not only power to achieve, but also strength to endure. In the face of stupendous tests He revealed unparalleled spiritual strength. Who else ever "endured such contradiction of sinners"? Once crucified in weakness and shame, He is now robed in strength and majesty. We join the angels in ascribing to Him—strength.

Honor. Honors in the realm of art or literature, music or science, sport or war are eagerly sought and highly prized. They are bestowed in just recognition of services rendered or excellence attained. But whose accomplishments can match the achievements of the Lamb? Who but He has redeemed from destruction men of every kindred and tongue and people and nation? True, on earth He experienced the deepest depths of dishonor in His death between two criminals. True, He refused to receive honor from men (John 5: 44). But an adoring universe delights to ascribe to Him the honor He is worthy to receive.

Glory. This word is more easy to illustrate than to define. It is something which belongs to God alone. It combines the ideas of splendor, radiance, renown. The noonday sun blinds us with the blaze of its glory. "We beheld his glory," wrote John of his vision of Christ on the Mount of Transfiguration when "his face did shine as the sun, and his raiment was white as the light" (Matt. 17:2). Of the same incident Peter wrote, "We . . . were eyewitnesses of his majesty" (II Pet. 1:16). The vision John had of Christ on Patmos was of One whose "countenance was as the sun shineth in his strength" (Rev. 1:16). John was yet to see the sun pale before the transcendent glory of the Lamb, for in Immanuel's land "the city had no need of the sun, neither of the moon, to shine in it, for the glory of God did lighten it, and the Lamb is the light thereof" (Rev. 21:23). The Lamb is worthy to receive—glory.

Blessing. Blessing is ascribed praise, a wish or prayer for happiness and success. It is the will to return thankful praise for favors received. "It is the one gift that we who have nothing can give to Him who possesses all." The least we can do is to return praise for blessings conferred. Although we cannot enrich the Lamb we can rejoice His heart by blessing His name. Limited though our concept of His glories may be, we can join the Psalmist in his ascription of praise: "Bless the Lord, O my soul: and all that is within me, bless His holy name" (Ps. 103:1).

But so magnanimous is the Lamb that while He graciously accepts our ascription to Him of these seven qualities, He refuses to enjoy them alone. He must share them with all who are united to Him by faith and love. All that He is, He is for us. All that He has, He shares with us.

Do we ascribe *power* to Him who has been given "all power in heaven and on earth"? Then He assures us, "Behold, I give unto you power . . . over all the power of the enemy" (Luke 10:19). Or *riches?* "He became poor, that ye through his poverty might be rich" (II Cor. 8:9). Or *wisdom?* "Christ . . . is made unto us wisdom" (I Cor. 1:30). Or strength? "I can do all things through Christ which strengtheneth me," testified Paul (Phil. 4:13). Or *glory?* "The glory which thou gavest me I have given them" (John 17:22). Or *honor?* "Them that honor me I will honor" (I Sam. 2:30). Or *blessing?* He "hath blessed us with all spiritual blessings" (Eph. 1:3). "Bless the Lord, O my soul."

THE GROUNDS OF THE ASCRIPTION

The Lamb will accept no honors He has not won, and this chapter gives solid grounds for the sevenfold ascription showing it to be our logical act of worship. The late Dr. F. B.

Meyer draws attention to five grounds for our ascription of worthiness.

His Sovereignty. "In the midst of the throne stood a Lamb," not sitting, but standing to rule His kingdom. Here Hebrews 2:9 has its fulfillment, "We see Jesus . . . crowned with glory and honor." No longer is He crowned with thorns, despised and rejected of men. In Him humanity has reached the throne of the universe and wields universal power.

> The highest place that heaven affords
>   He holds by sovereign right;
> As King of Kings and Lord of Lords
>   He reigns in glory bright.

His Character. "A Lamb . . ., having seven horns and seven eyes." No symbol occurs more frequently in Scripture than this, and none is more full of sacred significance. The word for "lamb" used here is found often in the Apocalypse, but in no other book is it applied to Christ. "It expresses endearment, the endearing relation in which Christ now stands to us, as the consequence of His previous relation as the sacrifical Lamb. So also our relation to Him. He the precious Lamb, we His dear lambs, one with Him" (Jamieson). Though clothed in majesty and glory, the Lamb is not an object of dread. If He has seven horns, symbol of His complete dominion over the world, He has also seven eyes, indicating the watchful care and wise providence of His Spirit over His people. In the Lamb there is a sublime combination of meekness and majesty, of mercy and might.

His Conquest. "The Lion of the tribe of Juda . . . hath prevailed to open the book, and to loose the seven seals thereof." Christ refused to be king by mere sovereign right or innate might as Son of God. He will gain and wear His crown as Son of man. When He stooped to become an infant, "He littered space with the glories He laid aside in His descent."

Hast thou not heard that my Lord Jesus died?
    Then let me tell you a strange story.
The God of power, when He did ride
    In His majestic robes of glory
Resolved to light, and so one day
He did descend, unrobing all the way.
    The stars His tire of light and rings obtained,
The clouds His bow, the fire His spear.
    The sky His azure mantle gained.
And when they asked what He did wear,
    He smiled and said as He did go,
    He had new clothes a-making down below.
               —GEORGE HERBERT

Entering the stream of our humanity and sharing all our sinless infirmities, step by step He fought His way back to the Throne. He was opposed at every step by the prince of darkness and his hosts. He went down to the grave, but He "death by dying slew." On the third day He returned, the keys of death and Hell hanging at His girdle. He conquered once and for all every power of evil.

His Sacrifice. "Thou art worthy . . . *for thou wast slain,* and hast redeemed us to God by thy blood out of every kindred, and tongue, and people, and nation." "It is not the Lion of the tribe of Judah," wrote W. M. Clow, "not the Lamb in His innocence and undisfigured beauty who takes the fast-closed book and breaks the seals, but the Lamb slaughtered. It is Christ in and by His cross who opens the book of God, gives the interpretation of the record and sets the hidden mysteries of providence and grace in clear light."

In the midst of the glories of Heaven, Christ crucified is central. We shall never be allowed to forget that we were not redeemed with shining silver or yellow gold, but with crimson drops of precious blood. The sentence pronounced on the first Adam was, "Thou shalt surely die." This sentence was exhausted on the last Adam: "Thou wast slain." His costly sacrifice was the climax of His glory, and because of it an adoring universe joins in an unending paean of praise.

His Achievement. "Thou hast made us unto our God kings and priests, and we shall reign on the earth." As the sacrificial Lamb He delivered us from the guilt and consequences of our sin. As the conquering Lion He met Satan in open conflict and defeated and disarmed him. He conquered sin and death and Hell. He regained His throne but He is unwilling to occupy it alone. He must share it with those He has redeemed. So He constitutes His people kings and priests—each a king who reigns with Him, each a priest ordained to offer the sacrifices of praise and thanksgiving continually. Small wonder that when the slain Lamb took the book and broke the seals, they sang a new song, a song in which we can and must join:

> Come, let us sing the song of songs,
>   The saints in heaven began the strain,
> The homage which to Christ belongs,
>   Worthy the Lamb, for He was slain.

THE UNFINISHED WORK OF CHRIST

"He ever liveth to make intercession" (Heb. 7:25)

READING: Hebrews 5:1-6; 7:22—8:1

WITHOUT CHRIST'S UNFINISHED WORK—His intercession at the Father's right hand—the benefits of His finished work on the Cross would never have reached us. The vast importance of that finished work can be gauged by the seemingly disproportionate space devoted in the Gospel records to the events surrounding His death. But Christ's costly work on Calvary would have been stillborn apart from the descent of the Holy Spirit at Pentecost and the presence of the Lord in Heaven. His unfinished ministry of intercession in Heaven is the capstone of His finished work on earth.

The heart of man, whether pagan or civilized, has ever craved a priest, a mediator who could represent him before his God. There seems to be a universal sense of a God who has been offended and must be appeased. There is the instinctive feeling that the one to set things right must be someone with compassion for human frailty and yet who has some special influence with God. In the dawn of history Job lamented, "Neither is there any daysman betwixt us, that might lay his hand upon us both" (9:33). This longing has resulted in the creation of orders of priests who men hoped could mediate with God on their behalf. Human priesthood reached its zenith in Judaism, but how imperfect a priesthood! Only in Christ, the Great High Priest, does this deep-seated yearning of humanity find complete satisfaction.

HIS QUALIFICATIONS AS HIGH PRIEST

The indispensable qualifications of the Jewish high priest were two. First, he must have *fellowship with man*, be linked to him by the ties of a common humanity. He must be "taken from among men" (Heb. 5:1). Only thus would he be able to have compassion on those he was to represent. He must be "able to have a moderated feeling" toward them, neither too lenient nor too severe. Compassion is essential to the idea of priesthood.

But human qualifications, though necessary, are not sufficient for such a delicate and exalted office. He must have *authority from God* for his ministry. The appointment must enjoy the Divine approval. "No man taketh this honor unto himself but he that is called of God, as was Aaron" (Heb. 5:4).

Does Christ meet these requirements? That He might help the race, He became part of it. He was indeed "*taken from among men*" and "in all things . . . made like unto his brethren" (Heb. 2:17). In order that His identification with man might be complete, He came as a working man, not as a king, but sharing the pinch of poverty and the cark of care. He enjoyed the heights of popularity and suffered the extremes of isolation. But at the same time He received *authority from God*. He was not self-elected, but was appointed by Him who said to Him, "Thou art my Son . . . Thou art a priest forever" (Heb. 5:5, 6).

Christ is morally and spiritually qualified to exercise His priestly ministry of intercession. "He ever liveth to make intercession for them. He "is holy, harmless, undefiled, separate from sinners, and made higher than the heavens" (Heb. 7:25, 26). He was born *holy* and lived a holy life. The word translated "holy" uniformly describes one who faithfully and meticulously does his duty to God. At the close of His life Jesus claimed, "I have glorified thee on the earth: I have finished the work thou gavest me to do" (John 17:4). He was *harmless*, guileless, never deceived or hurt any man, and therefore absolutely trustworthy. He was

undefiled, stainless, free from any blemish which would un-
fit Him for approach to God. He was *separate from sinners;*
not physically, for He constantly moved among them, but
morally separate. He was entirely different from them in
that while He experienced the full blast of temptations He
conquered them all and emerged without sin. He was *made
higher than the heavens,* exalted to the right hand of the
Majesty on high.

His Capabilities as High Priest

In this office Christ earns a triple honor.

He is able to succor. "Wherefore in all things it behooved
him to be made like unto his brethren, that he might be
a merciful and faithful high priest in things pertaining to
God, to make reconciliation [propitiation] for the sins of the
people. For in that he himself hath suffered being tempted,
he is able to succor them that are tempted" (Heb. 2:17, 18).
Being Himself truly human, He is able to meet man on the
plane of his need. We are very willing to aid those requiring help but so often we mourn our utter inability to do so.
Our High Priest knows no such limitation. It should be
noted that His ability to succor is grounded not in mere
pity but in costly propitiation (2:17). Because He has suffered in thus making propitiation for our sins, He is able to
succor us in our temptations and adequate to deal with our
sins and rebellion.

He is able to sympathize. We have not an High Priest
who is unable to sympathize with our weaknesses (Heb.
4:15). He never sympathizes with or condones our sin;
He condemns it. Sin always breaks fellowship with God
and sinning man needs an Advocate to keep the way open
through restoration. Because He has borne sin's penalty and
exhausted its judgment, He is able to cleanse when there is
heart confession.

Our Lord is able to sympathize with our infirmities and
weaknesses, which, though not sins, may easily degenerate

into sin. Sympathy is the ability to enter into the experiences of another as if they were one's own. It reaches its highest power where one has suffered the same experiences. Since Christ was "tempted in all points like as we are," and has felt the tremendous pressure of sin upon His own spirit without yielding to its allurement, He is able to enter sympathetically into the experiences of those passing through the fires of testing.

He is able to save. "He is able also to save them to the uttermost that come unto God by him, seeing that he ever liveth to make intercession for them" (Heb. 7:25). Because He thus lives forever as our Mediator and High Priest, He is able to bring to its final completion the salvation of all who draw near. The use of the present tense indicates "a sustained experience resulting from a continuous practice. 'He is able to be saving those who are continually coming,' *i.e.*, those who make it a regular habit to draw near to God" (A. M. Stibbs).

Save is a spacious word and is used in Scripture in varying senses. In Matthew's Gospel the word is used in four different but closely related senses: deliverance from the power of sin (1:21), deliverance from danger (8:25), deliverance from disease (9:21), and deliverance from the condemnation of God (10:23; 24:13). One expositor suggests that while in Romans salvation is from death, Hell and judgment, in Hebrews it is deliverance from the pressure of things about and within us, from all that obscures the vision of Christ. Our Intercessor is able to save us completely, in the most comprehensive meaning of the term. There is no personal problem to which He is not able to provide the solution, no sin from which He is not able to deliver, no enemy from which He is not able to rescue His trusting child. And why? Because "He ever liveth to make intercession for them." Having offered a complete and perfect sacrifice for sin, He has passed within the veil and appears in the presence of the Father as our Advocate and Intercessor.

AN ILLUSTRATION OF HIS INTERCESSION

"Jesus Christ the same yesterday, and today, and for ever" (Heb. 13:8). If this is so we can learn much from His ministry of intercession in the days of His flesh. Intercession is the act of pleading for another. Is it without significance that most of His prayers were intercessory in character? The only occasion on which He asserted His will in prayer was that we might be with Him and behold His glory" (John 17:24). Every other prayer of His was intercessory.

Luke records Jesus' moving words to Peter: "Simon, Simon, behold, Satan hath desired to have you [plural, *all you disciples*] that he may sift you as wheat: but I prayed for thee [singular, *Peter*], that thy faith fail not" (Luke 22:31, 32). What a strengthening assurance this is in the light of what ensued. Through His intercession, Peter's faith would not fail. It was intercession anticipating a need of which the subject was entirely unconscious. Peter had no inkling that he was about to be exposed to a fierce attack of Satan. In the event, Peter failed, but his faith did not fail. By this incident our Lord intended to teach that similar intercession was typical of His ministry on behalf of His children.

It is of more than passing interest that two different words are used to describe Christ's ministry as Intercessor, the first of which is illustrated by the above incident. Paul speaks of Christ as One "who maketh intercession for us." The term employed here is a picturesque word of rescue by one who "happens on" someone in trouble. It implies *presenting oneself unsought*. When need demands, He who neither slumbers nor sleeps comes to our aid unsought as He did to Peter. The other word occurs in I John 2:1: "We have an advocate with the Father, Jesus Christ the righteous," a paraclete, *one who comes in response to a call* of need or danger. He comes at our call, pleads our cause and restores us fully. So whether our need is conscious or unconscious, He ever lives to make intercession for us.

THE BASIS OF HIS INTERCESSION

Christ's intercession is grounded in His sacrifice on the Cross. The "It is finished" of Calvary provided the basis for His unfinished work of intercession so clearly foreshadowed in the Levitical day of atonement (Lev. 16). Once a year the high priest entered the Holy of Holies carrying blood and incense. The blood he sprinkled on the mercy seat. The incense he burned before the Lord on the coals in his censer. Even so our great High Priest after His ascension entered within the veil, presented the blood of His own sacrifice, accompanied by the fragrance of a life lived in absolute devotion to God, a sweet-smelling savor. This was *the climax of the incarnation*. Because the God-man, still bearing our humanity, represents us before the Father, we are accepted because of our union with Him, and can draw near to God with holy confidence. His very presence there is an unanswerable plea.

> Five bleeding wounds He bears
>   Received on Calvary.
> They pour effectual prayers,
>   They strongly plead for me.
> Forgive him, O forgive, they cry,
> Nor let that ransomed sinner die.
>
>   —CHARLES WESLEY

THE MODE OF HIS INTERCESSION

"It is vain to ask *how* in detail He thus acts for us," wrote Bishop Moule. "The essence of the matter is His union with His people and His perpetual presence in that union, with the Father, as the once slain Lamb."

In our thinking, intercession is often associated with tearful supplication or agonizing entreaty. It is sometimes misconceived as a means of overcoming the apparent reluctance of God, but such ideas are entirely foreign to the interces-

sion of Christ. He does not appear as suppliant before a
God who must be coaxed into granting the desired boon.
He appears as our Advocate, not to appeal for mercy on our
behalf, but to claim justice for us—what we are entitled
to in virtue of His sacrifice, what He has secured for us by
His Cross—from a God who is "faithful and *just* to forgive
us our sins."

His intercession is not vocal. It is not an audible saying of
prayers. In his great annual act of intercession, Aaron uttered not one word. The silence of the sanctuary was broken only by the tinkling of the golden bells on the hem of
his robe. On the day of atonement it was the blood that
spoke, not Aaron. It is the presence of our Intercessor, bearing in His body the evidence of His victory that speaks for
us.

Amintas was convicted of crimes against the Roman state
and was being tried for treason. Hearing of his plight, his
elder brother Aeschylus, who had lost an arm in the service
of his country, hastened to the court. Bursting into the room
he lifted his arm stump and, catching the eye of the judge,
he said, "Amintas is guilty, but for Aeschylus' sake he shall
go free." The judge acquitted him. Even so our Intercessor presents the tokens of His sufferings and the Judge says
of us, "They are guilty, but for My Son's sake they shall go
free."

> Jesus my great High Priest offered His blood and died;
> My guilty conscience seeks no sacrifice beside:
>   His powerful blood did once atone,
>   And now it pleads before the throne.

His intercession is in perpetuity as He represents us before the throne of God. "Now to appear in the presence of
God for us." On the Cross He died to obtain salvation for
us. Before the throne He lives to maintain us in salvation.
Is not this the significance of the statement, "We shall be
saved by his [risen] life" (Rom. 5:10)? We could not hold

out for a day in the Christian life were it not that He lives
for us now to impart to us "all things that pertain unto life
and godliness."

He receives and presents our prayers, mingling with our
imperfect petitions the incense of His own merits. "There
was given unto him much incense, that he should offer it
with the prayers of all saints upon the golden altar which
was before the throne" (Rev. 8:3). The prayers of all saints,
passing as they do through the mind and heart of One who
is always in harmony with the will and purposes of the Father, become His own as He presents them. Our prayers of
faith do not ascend alone, they are steeped in His merits and
because of that are mightily effectual.

> To all our prayers and praises,
>   Christ adds His sweet perfume,
> And love the altar raises
>   These odors to consume.

His intercession is personal. "He ever liveth to make intercession for us." This is His personal present occupation.
He does not delegate this ministry to Gabriel. He discharges
it Himself. He is never too busy to personally care for our
concerns. As on earth, so in Heaven, He is still One who
serves.

Our need of His intercession is unremitting. H. de Vries
writes in this connection, "There is an impression among
some believers that our Lord's intercession is required *only*
when we are in extreme need or danger as Peter was when
Satan desired to sift him as wheat, for then it was that Jesus
prayed for him that his faith should not fail. And this would
be correct if our Lord's intercession were like the city fire
department which is called upon for help only when the
house is on fire. The fact is that our house is always on fire
and therefore always in need of His intercession. There is
not a moment when we are not in need or danger, and therefore our Lord liveth evermore to make intercession for us.
His intercession never ceases and is always prevailing. The

very extent of our need and helplessness is the only limit to His intercession."

What confidence it should give us to know that at this very moment our great High Priest, One who knows our weakness and enters into our feelings, One who has passed through all phases of human life, is now appearing in the presence of God *for us,* able to keep in temptation, comfort in sorrow, succor in weakness. The realization of this glorious truth impelled the writer of the Hebrews to sum up his treatise on the high priesthood in these words:

"Now in connection with what we have been saying *the chief point is that we have a High Priest* who has taken His seat at the right hand of the throne of God's majesty in the heavens, and ministers in the Holy place" (Heb. 8:1, Knox), a ministry which will continue as long as our need remains.

CHRIST'S IDEAL OF CHARACTER

"Blessed are the poor in spirit" (Matt. 5:3)

READING: Matthew 5:1-11

IN STRIKING CONTRAST to the thunderings and threatenings of the law, the manifesto of Christ's kingdom commences with a benediction. Blessedness is the keynote. And yet the pathway to this blessedness leads His followers through strange and unexpected territory. In a few concise and vivid word pictures Jesus outlines the ideal life, an ideal which was a reflection of the supremely attractive life He lived among men. He was the embodiment and example of His own lofty teaching in this pungent and penetrating sermon.

Jesus was an authority on blessedness. He was the blessed man depicted in Psalm 1 and was therefore qualified to reveal the qualities and attitudes of which this blessedness was the reward. How different they are from what one would expect—poverty, mourning, hunger, thirst, reviling, persecution. There must surely be some mistake, for how can these bring blessedness? It is a common idea that blessedness flows from the possession of wealth, the absence of sorrow, the gratification of appetite, being well spoken of and kindly treated. Christ's teaching cut right across this popular concept of happiness and indicated that the very experiences we are eager to avoid are the ones conducive to the deepest joy and most to be coveted.

"Blessed" is a word which has been ennobled by its use in the New Testament. It is derived from the Greek "to speak well of," and is akin to our word "happy" which in English etymology goes back to hap, chance, good luck. Originally it was used of Greek gods and men, but connoted largely outward prosperity. Jesus invested the word with a new dimension, giving it the sense of spiritual prosperity which is the outcome of pure character and a correct sense of values. It has been variously translated as "to be envied, to be congratulated, to be superlatively happy, to be spiritually prosperous, to be enviably fortunate, to be radiantly joyous."

Of the eight characteristics with their compensations which He listed, the first four relate to *our attitude to God* and the last four to *our attitude to our fellow-men*. The first group are passive personal qualities, the second active social qualities. In his relations with his God, the superlatively happy man is conscious of

A SENSE OF INADEQUACY

"Blessed are the poor in spirit, for theirs is the kingdom of heaven." Note, poor in spirit, not poor-spirited. Not merely diffident, but renounced in spirit. He is emptied of self-reliance. There is no hint of self-sufficiency. He considers himself insignificant. With Paul he confesses, "I know that in me . . . dwelleth no good thing."

It was the habit of Principal Cairns, the Scottish theologian, to say, "You first, I follow." Once, on approaching the platform a great burst of applause greeted him. He stood aside and let the man behind him go first and began himself to applaud. He never dreamed the applause could be for him! Such is the blessed man.

It is significant that there are two words translated "poor." One refers to a laborer who is poor by reason of his circumstances, the other to a beggar who is poor by choice. The laborer has nothing superfluous; the beggar has nothing at all. It is the latter word, suggesting spiritual destitution, which is employed here. To be a beggar in spirit, to be bankrupt on the grace of God is an attitude to covet. The man of the world is proud of his independence and self-reliance. The blessed man like his Master confesses, "I can of mine own self do nothing." The typical attitude of the beggar is seen in Acts 3:5: "He gave heed unto them, *expecting to receive something of them*." This man is broken of pride, and his sense of inadequacy for the demands of life, his consciousness of having empty hands, throws him back on the illimitable resources of God. His attitude is the complete antithesis of that of the Laodiceans who boasted, "I am rich and increased with goods and have need of nothing." Such poverty inevitably leads to spiritual affluence. Though himself poor, the blessed man makes, many rich. He may not be a success by earthly standards but he enjoys the kingdom of Heaven.

A SENSE OF CONTRITION

"Blessed are they that mourn, for they shall be comforted." It is not the sorrow itself that is a blessed thing, but rather the comfort which God ministers to the sorrowing. There can be no comfort where there is no grief. "The man who knows nothing of sorrow is incomplete. One side of his nature has not been developed," wrote Archbishop Harrington Lees. "The happiness of the Gospel message is that it alone professedly deals with the common lot of sorrow, and gives the oil of joy for mourning. This is its initial undertaking: its final guarantee is 'no sorrow, nor crying.'"

The word "mourn" indicates a sorrow which begins in the heart, takes possession of the whole person, and is outwardly manifested. The special form of sorrow envisaged in this word is sorrow over spiritual failure or actual sin. The sense of spiritual poverty, of lukewarmness toward God, of distance from Him, of unlikeness to Christ inevitably leads to regret and contrition. The boasting and self-sufficient Pharisee did not mourn or beat his breast like the penitent publican, nor did he enjoy the experience of justification. The prodigal first recognized his abject poverty: "I perish with hunger"; then in true contrition he acknowledged his sin: "Father, I have sinned." It was only when Job had a vision of God that he said in deep self-abasement, "I abhor myself and repent in dust and ashes." He mourned over what might have been had he not been self-satisfied.

The paradoxical thing about this mourning is that it is not incompatible with rejoicing. Paul claimed to be sorrowful, yet always rejoicing. The enjoyment of the comfort which God imparts to the contrite spirit is another of the ingredients of the superlatively happy life.

A SENSE OF MODESTY

"Blessed are the meek, for they shall inherit the earth." Meekness is not an invertebrate virtue, says one writer. It is not weakness or mere mildness of disposition, for our Lord claimed it as an element of His character, to be emulated by His disciples. Moses was meek (Num. 12:3) but he certainly was not weak. It is the gentleness of strength in reserve, not of effeminacy. Meekness can fight with strength and vigor when the glory of God or the interests of the kingdom are at stake. It was the meek and lowly Jesus who with upraised whip of cords expelled the mercenary traders from His Father's house. Nor is meekness mere good-naturedness which will take anything from anybody. Essentially it is that attitude of mind which does not insist on its own rights and is always ready to waive its privileges in the interests of others. It is always ready to renounce its own plans and to joyously embrace God's plans. Nietzsche preached that the world is ours if we can get it. Jesus preached that the world is ours if we *renounce* it; it is the meek, not the aggressive, who inherit the earth.

Of all qualities of character, meekness is probably the one least coveted. But Jesus extols it as a grace highly esteemed by God. "The ornament of a meek and quiet spirit, which is in the sight of God of great price" (I Pet. 3:4). The meek person is generally regarded as too good to make his way or count for much. Jesus refutes this concept by stating that it is he who inherits the earth. He is characterized too by a willingness to yield to others when principle is not at stake. He claims nothing but the whole earth is his.

A SENSE OF DESIRE

"Blessed are they which do hunger and thirst after right-eousness: for they shall be filled." One version renders it, "Blessed are they that are starving for righteousness, for they shall be crammed full." Jesus uses these elemental human instincts to illustrate the passionate desire for holiness and likeness to Christ which commands the full response of God. These are the most intense and agonizing human appetites when denied satisfaction. When Sir Ernest Shackleton and his party were left without food for some time during one of their journeys in the Antarctic, he said it was extremely difficult to think of anything else but food. The person who has an unquenchable thirst, an insatiable hunger, for a holy life, is one to be envied. Blessed starvation!

> As pants the hart for cooling streams
>   When heated in the chase,
> So pants my soul for Thee, my God,
>   And Thy redeeming grace.

It is noteworthy that the beatitude does not speak of hun-gering and thirsting after *happiness*. Happiness is the object of pursuit of the vast bulk of mankind but generally it proves only an elusive mirage. Jesus teaches here that when a man makes the primary object of his pursuit not happiness but *righteousness*—a right relationship with God—he obtains su-perlative happiness to boot. "They shall be filled"—to reple-tion, both here and hereafter. "He satisfieth the longing soul, and filleth the hungry soul with goodness" (Ps. 107:9).

From indicating the ideal attitude of the subjects of His kingdom toward God, Jesus turns to his social relationships with his fellows. The man who is spiritually prosperous ex-hibits a fourfold disposition in testing circumstances—"strength with weakness at its mercy, purity in contact with defiling company, love which sees others at variance, recti-tude suffering at the hands of tormentors. Each has its own beatitude, the fruit of a work of Divine grace."

A COMPASSIONATE SPIRIT

"Blessed are the merciful: for they shall obtain mercy." This beatitude has been correctly described as a self-acting law of the moral world. It is the man who shows mercy who receives mercy. We reap what we sow. It is possible for a man to hunger and thirst after righteousness, but for his righteousness to be hard and exacting. That quaint evangelist, Sam Jones, used to say that righteousness without mercy results in the indigestion countenance.

Like meekness, mercy is a distinctively Christian virtue and was little known among non-Christian people. It has its source in a compassionate feeling and is expressed in the compassionate act. Mercy is shown to those who have no claim on it. If they have a claim to mercy, then it is only justice they receive. The man of a compassionate spirit is always ready to make allowances for those who have failed, or to put the best construction on ambiguous behavior. He does not judge harshly, remembering that he is not in possession of all the facts. We do well to bear in mind that our experience is only the rebound of our attitude. Mercy knows no retaliation.

A CLEAN HEART

"Blessed are the pure in heart: for they shall see God." The beatific vision is vouchsafed on earth only to those of pure heart. Purity here is an inclusive term employed in its widest meaning—purity of thought, imagination, motive, act. It signifies moral holiness or integrity, and refers especially to one who is without guile. Jesus bypassed mere external and ceremonial purity and enforced the absolute necessity of inner purity. Outward conformity to ceremonial requirements satisfies the heart of neither God nor man.

"Create in me a clean heart, O my God," pleaded David in contrition, deeply conscious of his impurity and sin against his fellow-men. The Psalmist connected clean hands with a pure heart, recognizing his responsibility in human attitudes and relationships. There is no such thing as clearness of vision where there is not cleanness of heart. Too many are satisfied with outward presentability. They do not mind minor deviations from the path of moral rectitude so long as they can evade "losing face" with their own circle. The Divine dictum is, "Without holiness no man shall see the Lord." There is a daily need of self-examination and appropriation of the cleansing of the blood of Christ.

To see God involves moral not physical vision, for God is Spirit. Sin beclouds the heart and obscures the face of God. To see God is to know God, to enjoy intimate fellowship with Him. Hypocrisy and insincerity are ruled out if one is to see God in this sense. With Christ in the heart as the indwelling fountain of purity, the maintenance of a clean heart becomes a glorious possibility. When this is experienced, it is possible to anticipate here on earth the day when we shall see Him face to face.

A CONCILIATORY MINISTRY

"Blessed are the peacemakers: for they shall be called the children of God." This beatitude is often read as though it referred to peacekeepers—keepers of a peace which was already in existence—or to peaceable men. Instead it refers to the one who makes peace in a situation where that peace has been broken. It is not a virtue, but an activity which is in view. Making peace is a much more costly ministry than maintaining peace. Our Lord "made peace by the blood of his cross." We can make peace only by allowing our own peace to be broken. There is always a cross in this ministry. In the presence of such a person, quarrels and discord die away. It was said of a noted British statesman, that when he came into the House, no matter how bitter the debate or wrangling, it always withered away in his presence. And why? He lived in the presence of God. No matter how late the House sat, he always spent two hours in prayer and devotion before embarking on the work of the day. He carried the peace of God with him and radiated it wherever he went. This is a ministry which calls for un-

common courage and insight and tact. But what a ministry
it is to bring together those who have been estranged. Paul
used all his skill and tact in his endeavor to heal the breach
between Euodias and Syntyche, as recorded in his Philippian
letter (4:2).

The reward for the peacemaker is not to *become* a child
of God but to *be called* a child of God. He is already a child
of God. It is not his pedigree but his reputation that is in
view. As people see him going about his costly ministry of
bringing peace, they see in him the image of his Master and
recognize the family likeness.

A COURAGEOUS LOYALTY

"Blessed are they that are persecuted for righteousness'
sake . . . when men shall revile you, and persecute you, and
say all manner of evil against you falsely, for my sake. Rejoice, and be exceeding glad: for great is your reward in
heaven." Even a peacemaker is not immune from the as-
saults and persecutions of his fellow-men. The sinless Christ
was not exempt from persecution and reviling. But note
that the blessedness does not lie in the persecution or reviling. It is they that *have been persecuted*—for this is the correct tense—who *are* superlatively happy. It is the "afterward" of chastening. The blessedness consists in the joy of
the special nearness of Christ in the time of trial. The man
who is enviably fortunate, like the three young men in the
burning fiery furnace, discovers that in the midst of the
fierce fires of persecution, the Son of God walks with him
and the fire does not kindle on him.

It must be observed, however, that all persecution does
not bring this blessedness. There are three qualifying conditions. It must be

Persecution "for righteousness' sake" (v. 10), not because
of our own angularity or unwisdom. Many Christians bring
unnecessary opprobrium upon themselves and the cause of
Christ by their aggressive tactlessness. The persecution in

view here comes upon us because we will do right at all costs, even if it results in social ostracism.

Reviling falsely based (v. 11), not which has been deserved. It is reviling which has no justification in either our words or actions which brings blessedness.

Persecution and reviling "for my sake" (v. 11). Ill treatment which arises from our loyalty to Christ and His righteousness will bring its own magnificent reward. The sharing of His sufferings is deeply appreciated by our Master. "Be glad and supremely joyful, for your reward in Heaven is strong, intense." This must have been a strikingly new concept to the Jews, who generally considered suffering and persecution as a curse from God.

Such is our Lord's lofty concept of ideal Christian character. Is it ours? Is it too high? God knows no standard but the character of His Son. He purposes that we should all be conformed to the image of His Son, and it is the delight of the Holy Spirit to bring this about.

CHRIST'S TERMS OF DISCIPLESHIP

"Come to me. . . . Come after me. . . ." Luke 14:26, 27

READING: Luke 14:25-33

THE NEW TESTAMENT is shot through with instruction on discipleship and its implications. It bulked largely in the teaching of our Lord but has been neglected or toned down in the teaching of His church. The reason is not far to seek. No teaching of Christ was more unpopular and unwelcome in His day, and succeeding years have seen little change in the human heart. The terms He laid down for thoroughgoing discipleship were so stringent that the crowds melted away from Him when they perceived its costliness.

Jesus was presented with a unique opportunity of capitalizing on the great popularity He had gained in recent months. "There went great multitudes with him" who hung on His every word. How will He improve this most favorable situation? Will He perform some sensational sign to further excite their curiosity? Will He flatter them to draw out their adulation? Will He offer some special inducement or indulgence to secure their allegiance? Instead, He seemed intent on alienating their sympathy by laying down conditions which appeared unnecessarily hard. A strange type of leadership this, to deliberately discourage those whose support He would surely be anxious to gain! We tend to scale down our demands in order to win the crowd. Jesus purposefully made following Him desperately hard and deliberately thinned the crowd of would-be disciples (see Luke 9:57-62).

In terms unmistakably clear, Christ indicated that being His disciple involved far more than an easy assent to a creed.

107

It would be costly and exacting rather than thrilling and exciting. Instead of representing discipleship as easy and delightful, He emphasized its difficulties and dangers. He spoke more of the foes that would be encountered than of the friends who would be enjoyed. Not of silver slippers and primrose paths, but of rocky roads and shoes of iron. Never did He throw out a bait to secure a recruit, never concealed the cost of being His disciple. Everyone who followed Him would do so with eyes wide open. Browning correctly interpreted the teaching of our Lord.

> How very hard it is to be a Christian!
> Hard for you and me;
>   Not the mere task of making real
>   That duty up to its ideal,
> Effecting thus, complete and whole,
> A purpose of the human soul,
>   For that is always hard to do.

Dynamic leaders have always been alive to the fact that the finest response is made when the hardest challenge is presented. When Garibaldi was setting out to deliver his country from an invading horde, he encountered a group of idle young fellows and invited them to join him in his crusade. "What do you offer us?" they demanded. "Offer you? I offer you neither pay nor quarters nor provisions. I offer hunger, thirst, forced marches, battle, death. Let him who loves his country in his heart, not with his lips only, follow me." They followed him. The missionary enterprise has always been marked by discomfort and privation, hardship and danger in the noblest of all causes, and yet the imagination of youth has always been captured by the call to sacrifice.

The term "disciple" means "learner." But implicit in the word is the idea of one who learns with the purpose of translating the lessons into action. A Christian disciple is a voluntary learner in the school of Christ. Jesus first invites, "Come unto me," and then follows it with "Come after me." But not all who come to Him for salvation are willing to come after Him in sacrifical service. Though they ought to be, "disciple" and "believer" are not in practice synonymous terms.

J. Edgar Hoover, head of the Federal Bureau of Investigation in Washington, affirms that Communism always stresses the relationship between theory and action. "To study the Communist 'masters' is to ready oneself for revolutionary action. Communists are not interested in preparing members to parade their Marxist IQ's or pass academic examinations. Their knowledge must become a weapon to turn the world upside down for Communism. 'We study,' they say, 'for the sole purpose of putting into practice what we have learned. It is for the Party and for the victory of the revolution that we study.' " Mr. Hoover pertinently asks, "Are we as Christians adapting to actual practice the teachings of Christ? Are our day to day actions in the secular world determined by our Christian beliefs?"

Why did our Lord make His terms of discipleship so exacting, when the inevitable result would be the loss of popular support? Because He was concerned more with *quality* than with *quantity*. He desired a band of picked men and women, a Gideon's band, on whose unwavering devotion He could count in days of crisis. He wanted trustworthy disciples on whom He could rely when building His church or battling with the powers of evil (Luke 14:29, 31). Once the disciple is convinced of the majesty and the glory of the Christ he follows and of the cause in which he is enlisted, he will be willing for any sacrifice.

Several centuries ago an invading Eastern king whose march had met with unbroken success, neared the territory of the young chieftain Abu Taber. Hearing of his valor, the king was reluctant to kill him and instead sent an ambassador with terms of peace. When he heard the proposal, Abu Taber summoned one of his soldiers, handed him a dagger and commanded, "Plunge this into your breast." The soldier obeyed and fell dead at his feet. Calling another he ordered, "Leap over that precipice into the Euphrates." Without a moment's hesitation he leaped to his death. Turning to the ambassador Abu said, "Go, tell your master I have five hundred men like that, and that within twenty-four hours I will have him chained with my dogs." The king with his greatly superior numbers continued his advance, but numbers were of no avail against the fierce loyalty of Abu Taber's devotees. Before a day had passed the king was chained with Abu's dogs. It is quality that is important.

Christianity truly interpreted has never been popular. Indeed a religion that is popular is far removed from the teaching of our Lord. "Woe unto you, when all men shall speak well of you! for so did their fathers to the false prophets," He warned (Luke 6:26). On the contrary, the Christian is truly blessed when men revile him and say all manner of evil against him falsely for Christ's sake (Matt. 5:11). We are invited to share, not His popularity but His unpopularity. "Let us go forth therefore unto Him without the camp, bearing his reproach" (Heb. 13:13). We are to expect that "all who will live godly shall suffer persecution," not enjoy popular favor. We are invited to share "the fellowship of His sufferings" rather than to bask in His reflected glory. If we experience little of the "offence of the cross," it is because we, like Peter, are following Christ "afar off."

With utter sincerity Jesus affirmed, "Strait is the gate, and narrow is the way, which leadeth unto life, and few there be that find it," so we need not be surprised if the way of full discipleship is not crowded. Teaching such as this soon thins the crowd and eliminates the superficial. "As long as the church wore scars," said Vance Havner, "they made headway. When they began to wear medals, the cause languished. It was a greater day for the church when Christians were fed to the lions than when they bought season tickets and sat in the grandstand."

In His discourse, our Lord spoke of "counting the cost." There are two interpretations of this reference. One is that would-be disciples should carefully count the cost before they embark on the exacting road of discipleship. This is of course true, and is emphasized in the three irreducible claims of Christ which are the pith of the paragraph. But there is a strong body of opinion that the only way in which the passage reads logically and coherently is that it is Christ who is the tower-builder, Christ who is the campaigning King. It is He who is doing the calculating and counting the cost. Can He afford to use as His builders and soldiers those whose commitment to Him is merely nominal and not sacrifical? The issues involved are so stupendous that He can afford to number me among His disciples only if I comply with His conditions, only if I am willing to follow Him to the death.

He enunciates three indispensable conditions of discipleship.

Touching the heart's affections—an unrivaled love. "If any man come to me, and hate not his father, and mother, and wife, and children, and brethren, and sisters, yea, and his own life also, he *cannot* be my disciple" (v. 26). We can be His disciples only if we love Him better than anyone else. Following Him involves a clash of loyalties. His incoming is divisive. Inevitably there come the contrasting claims of kin and Christ, and in the realm of the heart's affection Christ tolerates no rival.

"Hate" as used here sounds harsh and arbitrary, but the word is used in a relative, not in the absolute sense. It means simply "to love less." The unbalanced zealot will find no excuse here for a lack of natural affection. Jesus does not contradict Himself. There is no conflict between this demand and the command to honor father and mother. In the days when He spoke these words, becoming His disciple involved a man in discord with his family and ostracism by society. In Western lands there is little family or social cost involved, but this is far from the case on the mission fields. Declaring allegiance to Christ may involve a man in the loss of employment, of wife and children, even of life itself. And yet Christ does not scale down His demands.

Jesus was no ruthless iconoclast. He commanded filial and marital and parental love, but He knew that often "a man's foes are they of his own household." The crucial test is, will natural affection prevail over love to Him? In every crisis, love for Him must win the day if we are to be His disciples. The fact is that when He is thus given the pre-eminent place in our affections, every human relationship is enriched. Because we love Him more, it by no means follows that we will love our own kin less. The reverse is the case.

He further demands that love for Him shall triumph over our instinctive love of ourselves. "Yea, and his own life also." The condition passes over from the family circle to the central citadel of a man's own life. Christ is concerned that our deeply entrenched self-life shall be superseded once and for all. With Paul, the disciple will be able to say, "Neither count I my life dear unto myself."

If there is in our hearts no such unrivaled love for Christ, He affirms that we *cannot* be His disciples.

Touching life's conduct—an unceasing cross-bearing. "Whosoever doth not bear his cross, and come after me, *cannot* be my disciple" (v. 27).

Ramon Lull, the earliest missionary to the Moslems, tells how he became a missionary. He had been living a luxurious and pleasure-loving life. One day while he was alone Christ came to him carrying His cross and saying, "Carry this for Me." But he pushed Him off and refused. Again when he was in the silence of a great cathedral Christ came; again He asked him to carry His cross and again he refused. Christ came a third time, and this time, said Lull, "He took His cross and without a word left it lying in my hands. What could I do but take it up and carry it?" He did so, but it issued in his being stoned to death.

What did Christ mean by "his cross"? Certainly not physical infirmity, or temperamental weakness, or misfortune, trouble, or disease. These are unavoidable and are the common lot of all humanity, whether Christian or non-Christian. The fact that our Lord preceded His statements with His hypothetical "if" indicates that something voluntary is involved. In simplest terms, the Cross stands for shame and suffering and death. It is a symbol of rejection by the world. Obviously, a real identification with Christ in the shame and suffering of His Cross is implied. Bearing our own cross is a matter of choice. It is not thrust on us as was Jesus' cross on Simon of Cyrene. It signifies a willingness to share the scorn, the hatred, the ostracism of the world for His sake. A worldly disciple would be a contradiction in terms. Paul knew what was involved in this identification with a crucified Christ. "Being reviled, we bless; being persecuted, we suffer it: being defamed, we entreat: we are made as the filth of the world, and are the offscouring of all things unto this day" (I Cor. 4:12, 13).

When we voluntarily embrace the adverse circumstances of life as instruments of death to the selfish and self-centered existence, we are bearing our own cross. Received aright, the sufferings, the limitations and trials of life will lead us to our true position as crucified with Christ. "Whoso looketh on the white side of Christ's cross and taketh it up handsomely, shall find it to him just such a burden as wings are to a bird" (Samuel Rutherford).

If we are unwilling for unceasing cross-bearing, we *cannot* be His disciples.

Touching personal possessions—an unqualified renunciation. "Whosoever he be of you that forsaketh not *all* that he hath, *cannot* be my disciple" (v. 33). Our Lord's third requirement for discipleship is a full surrender of all, not a fine surrender of much. "All that he hath," are His words. In the Amplified New Testament, the word "forsake" is expanded thus: "renounce, surrender claim to, give up, say goodby to." It is the absoluteness of our Lord's demand which is so staggering. It admits of no exceptions. He claims the right to dispose of everything in His disciple's possession as He in His wise love sees best.

With most people possessions, goods, property very easily

become objects of love and devotion. "Things" can exercise a terrible tyranny over us. But we cannot serve God and mammon, we cannot give allegiance to two masters. Where the heart is divided between dual interests, discipleship is impossible. The lesson the Master was seeking to teach is that we are trustees of our possessions, not owners.

Discipleship will not necessarily involve a literal selling of all our possessions and giving away the proceeds, but it does not preclude such a possibility. The disciples claimed, "We have left *all* and followed thee." Paul said, "I suffer the loss of *all* things." Of the early church it was said, "Neither said any of them that *aught* of the things which he possessed was his own; but they had *all* things common" (Acts 4:32). Whatever else is involved in this condition, it means there must be such a real and deliberate renunciation and giving up our claim to all that we have, as will forever set us free from covetousness and selfishness. Our Master expects us to hold all that we have in a relaxed, inverted hand and not in a tightly clenched fist. Our attitude will be, "Lord, help Yourself to whatever You wish of mine."

Otherwise, we *cannot* be His disciples.

For obedience to these three unequivocal demands, some powerful motive is necessary. It is found in Christ's own example. He asks nothing of us He was not willing to do Himself. For love of us He "hated" His Father and His heavenly home, and came as the sinless God-man to live in a world of sin where often He had not where to lay His head. For our sake, Jesus "bearing his cross went to . . . Golgotha . . . where they crucified him" (John 19:17, 18). For our eternal enrichment He renounced all that He had. "Though he was rich, yet for your sakes he became poor, that ye through his poverty might be rich" (II Cor. 8:9). Is the servant greater than his Lord? Shall we be reluctant to do for Him what He so willingly did for us? When we fulfill these three conditions, then and only then are we His disciples indeed.

A PERSONAL LETTER FROM CHRIST

"Unto the angel of the church at Ephesus, write . . ."
(Revelation 2:1)

READING: Revelation 2:1-7

A PERSONAL LETTER from the exalted Christ to a living church is indeed a memorable document and it is a high privilege to be able to share its message. Though primarily directed to the church of Ephesus, it concludes with an individual and contemporary appeal, "He that hath an ear, let him hear . . ." In it there is appreciation tinged with pathos, commendation tempered by condemnation. Christ represents Himself as the One who walks among the seven golden lampstands, which in 1:20 are identified as the seven churches. He oversees and scrutinizes the shining of their lamp of witness. In His letter He passes moral judgment on the church from the vantage point of full and accurate knowledge. "I know thy works."

Ephesus was one of the notable cities of ancient times. Its citizens called it the metropolis of Asia. It was wealthy and cultured but utterly corrupt. Besides being an important commercial center, it was the focus of a vile form of heathen worship. It boasted the magnificent temple of Diana, one of the seven wonders of the world, which brought both wealth and notoriety. The church in Ephesus was uniquely privileged in the galaxy of spiritual gift possessed by its founder and successive pastors. Paul, Apollos, Priscilla and Aquila, Timothy and John had each contributed to its spiritual life. That they responded to and grasped the deep spiritual teaching they received is clear from the heights of spiritual truth to which Paul rises in his letter to them. The type of believer forming the nucleus of the church can best be gauged by the spiritual teaching they were able to assimilate.

By the time this letter was penned the Ephesian church had been established for forty years and its membership was of second and third generation Christians. The sublime new truths which had enraptured their forbears had now become commonplace. But much of the stability and strength of the previous generation was still in evidence, and for this Christ expresses His warm appreciation.

COMMENDATION

The tact and understanding of the Master stands out in clear relief in the opening sentence of His letter. It is noteworthy that when He has something to commend, He mentions that first, always a sound procedure in human relationships. He commended them without qualification for four virtues manifest in their midst.

They were *loyal in labor*. "I know thy works, and thy labor and thy patience" (v. 2). The whole life and conduct of the church is in view here, sacrificial toil and unflagging patience in the midst of weariness. The church was a hive of industry, full of good works. There was nothing passive about their patience. It was persistence in toil even to the point of exhaustion, and for this Christ warmly commended them. It is worthy of note that the three words used in this sentence occur also in Paul's letter to the Thessalonians where he commends their "*work* of faith, and *labor* of love, and *patience* of hope" (I Thess. 1:3).

Then, too, they were *intolerant of impostors*. "Thou canst not bear them that are evil" (v. 2). This was a church which would not condone impurity of any kind in its midst. There was sufficient spiritual virility to exercise a wholesome discipline, and for this they received Divine commendation. The Ephesian church could bear anything except the presence of impostors in its midst.

As a church they were *discerning in doctrine*. "Thou hast tried them which say they are apostles, and are not, and hast found them liars" (v. 2). From the tense of the verb it would appear that our Lord was referring to a recent crisis in which they had tested the doctrine of the Nicolaitans (v. 6) who posed as equal or even superior to the original apostles, and had condemned them. Forewarned by Paul in his farewell address (Acts 20:29), they had been on the watch for the "grievous wolves" to which he alluded. Here were believers who were careful of what they listened to and they were not deceived. But not only did they test their words, they tested their deeds also, and rejected them. For this Christ, who is the Truth, commended them. "Thou hatest the deeds of the Nicolaitans, which I also hate" (v. 6). Ignatius bore this testimony to the Ephesian church: "Ye live according to the truth and no heresy hath a home among you: nay ye do not so much as listen to anyone if he speak of aught else save concerning Jesus Christ."

Finally, they were *patient in persecution*. "[Thou] hast borne, and hast patience, and for my name's sake hast labored, and hast not fainted" (v. 3). In the midst of raging fires of persecution they had displayed a remarkable staying power.

With such an amazing and deserved commendation from the Christ, whose "eyes were as a flame of fire," this church surely has grounds for self-congratulation. What more could be expected of her? How gratified we would be if all our churches merited such praise. But Christ's penetrating eye saw a fatal defect beneath the fair exterior. His listening ear detected a missing note in the harmony of its worship.

COMPLAINT

"Nevertheless I have somewhat against thee, because thou hast left thy first love"—you have abandoned the love you had at the first. The prophetic word of the Lord Jesus had already come true (Matt. 24:12). At first blush this may not seem a matter of tremendous importance against the background of their many admirable qualities, but such a view is terribly superficial. Is it a small thing to a wife if her husband abandons the love he had for her at the first? A beautiful home, a large bank account, good social position would be as ashes to her if he withdrew his love. No suffering is so poignant as that of unrequited love.

It would appear that some crisis had come in the history of this loyal, busy, orthodox church which had caused their early love for Christ to wane. Had they become so ardent in the consuming task of maintaining good works that their love for Christ had cooled off? Were they so busy hating the deeds of the Nicolaitans that they had ceased to love Christ? Loss of love for Christ is no trifle. The work and labor and patience of the newly converted Thessalonian Christians each had an inspiring motive—faith, love, hope. But for the second generation Ephesian believers, faith and love and hope had fallen by the way, and all that was left was work, labor, patience. Without the inspiring motives their work became a burden and their orthodoxy a dead thing. It takes ardent love for Christ to make these activities of lasting spiritual value. Toil and zeal and even self-sacrifice are no substitute for love.

Men do not think loss of love for Christ a very serious thing, but He views it as a sin of such terrible dimensions that unless it is repented of, it would result in the destruction of the witness of the church. It would have failed in the very purpose for which it was brought into being.

COUNSEL

First the exalted Christ calls on the church to *remember*. "Remember therefore from whence thou art fallen" (v. 5). There is a time to look backward and a time to look forward. Memory can exercise a salutary ministry when it is brought into play. We have a fatal facility for forgetting unpleasant or unwelcome facts or truths. If we love Christ less today than we did in the early days of our new life, He says we have fallen. We may not have fallen into gross sin, but we have fallen out of love with Christ. Let us think back to see if there was a time when our love for Christ was more passionate, more sacrificial than it is today. "Remember" is in the imperative mood and our Master is commanding us to put our memories to work. It is true that love is likely to be more demonstrative in its early stages than later, but as love matures it will run ever deeper and more strongly. Has this been our experience?

Jeremiah's prophecy has a poignant paragraph. "The word of the Lord came to me, saying, Go and cry in the ears of Jerusalem, saying, Thus saith the Lord; I remember thee, the kindness of thy youth, the love of thine espousals, when thou wentest after me in the wilderness, in a land that was not sown" (Jer. 2:1-2). God remembered with sad joy the glow and warmth of His people's early love for Him, a love which was then selfless and sacrificial. But now that glow had faded. He recalled with wistful grief its four beautiful characteristics.

He remembered *the kindness of their love.* "I remember the kindness of thy youth," the early days when they loved Him more than anyone or anything else; when they showed a sensitive and solicitous concern for His feelings; when they considered and consulted Him in everything large and small. The touchstone of all activity was, "Will this please Him?" Has the center of our life shifted so that the question has become, "Will this please me?" Correctness of relationship does not take the place of the kindness of love.

The devotion of their love in early courtship was fresh in His memory. "I remember the love of thine espousal." Newly awakened love is a very beautiful thing. When Hudson Taylor was traveling by train in France, a young and obviously newly married couple entered his compartment. They were entirely oblivious of their fellow-traveler. The bride could hardly take her eyes from her lover's face. She anticipated every wish. They were entirely absorbed in each other. Mr. Taylor said, "My heart cried out, O that I had such a love for my Lord!"

God recalled with deep appreciation *the exclusiveness of*

their love. "Thou wentest after *Me.*" He was the center of their world and around Him everything revolved. Personal devotion to Him motivated their whole life. But now "*Me*" had degenerated into "*It.*" It is perilously easy for devotion to the Lord's Person to deteriorate into devotion to the Lord's work.

Ramon Lull, the Spanish nobleman and brilliant university professor of the thirteenth century, turned from his alluring prospects to evangelize the Moslems. Twice he was banished from the country. He spent a year and a half immured in a dungeon. As an old man, when taken to a wall and stoned to death, his last words were, "Jesus only." Shortly before he died he said, "He that loves not lives not, and he that lives by Christ shall never die." The terms of his consecration vow were, "To Thee, O Lord God, I offer myself, my wife, my children, and all I possess," and to his dying day he never revoked the exclusiveness of his love for Christ.

When persecution was raging in Holland, Geleyn de Muler was told to recant and give up reading the Bible or suffer death by fire. He had a wife and four children. "Do you love your wife and children?" asked Titelman. "God knows that were the heaven a pearl and the earth a globe of gold, and were I owner of all, most cheerfully would I give them up for my family, even though our fare be only bread and water. *But not for Christ.*" He was strangled and burned.

God was not forgetful of *the sacrifice of their love.* "Thou wentest after me in the wilderness, in a land that was not sown." Theirs was an uncalculating love, a love which was prepared for risks. In the glow of their first devotion they were willing to sacrifice everything if only they could be with Him, for the one thing love cannot endure is distance. Loneliness, privation, hunger, poverty held no terrors if they had the compensation of His presence. There is not much to allure in a wilderness, the place of temptation and testing. It was a "land not sown," with no security, no prospects; but this could not quench the ardor of their love. There was no certainty of harvest and no assurance for the future, yet

in spite of this they followed Him there. He remembered
with deep joy the kindness of a love that renounced all other
loves and prospects simply to be with Him.

Next Christ called on the church at Ephesus to *repent*
(v. 5). He issues an imperative demand for an immediate
change of mind, attitude and conduct before it is too late.
It is a word which combines the intellectual and the volition-
al. It was not sufficient for the Ephesians to feel badly
about their sin of having fallen out of love with Christ, they
had to fall in love with Him afresh, and this was in their
power to do. The expression, "thou didst leave thy first love"
almost implies some crisis, some definite point of time when
the chilling wind began to blow. Pilgrim found the lost roll
exactly where he left it. It may be that for some of us it will
be necessary to take a mental pilgrimage to the occasion
when we lost the love we had at the first.

Finally, He calls on them to *reform*. "Do at once the
works you did at the first." Again it is an imperative. They
are to resume the works they used to do, and the implication
is that the change of mind toward Christ coupled with a
renewal of the former activities which then sprang from a
glowing love for Christ, would once again kindle the fire of
love in the heart. Love is a matter of the will as well as of
the emotions. When adjustment is corrected, love will return again.

Christ enforced His commands with a solemn warning.
"Repent, and do the first works; or else I will come unto thee
quickly, and will remove thy candlestick out of its place,
except thou repent" (v. 5). Apparently this appeal was
effective for a period, and love for Christ was again apparent in the Ephesian church, but not for long. The lamp
of witness guttered out and history tells the sequel. Ephesus
is now only a squalid village set in the ruins of her former
glory, and Christian testimony is nonexistent. Trench records a visitor to the village finding only three Christians
there, and these so ignorant that they had hardly heard the
names of Paul or John.

This letter has a contemporary message and warning to the church of our day. Where other things are magnified and fostered in the life of the church at the expense of fervent love for Christ, the congregation may remain intact but the lampstand has in reality been removed—having a name to live, but dead.

COMPENSATION

The letter does not close on a negative note. It began with commendation, it ends with compensation. "To him that overcometh will I give to eat of the tree of life, which is in the midst of the paradise of God" (v. 7). Here is a glorious promise to the one who is obedient to the exhortation and warning of his Lord. He who overcomes receives something better than the food offered to idols with which the Ephesian believers were tempted. He will have free access to the tree of life which was forbidden to Adam in Eden. He will be given to eat of the tree of life—to feed on Christ Himself. What man lost in the primal sin in Eden is gloriously restored to the overcomer in any age.

A REIGNING LIFE THROUGH CHRIST

"It is a far greater thing that through another Man, Jesus Christ, men by their acceptance of His more than sufficient grace and righteousness should live all their lives like kings" (Romans 5:17, Phillips)

READING: Romans 5:12-21

LIVING ALL THEIR LIVES LIKE KINGS." What an alluring picture of the Christian life Paul presents in these few words! And when he wrote of kings he was not referring to a limited constitutional monarchy such as we know today. Now the king or queen is largely a symbol, while executive power is vested in Parliament and prime minister. Then, the king possessed absolute and despotic powers which were beneficent if he was a good man, tyrannical if he was a bad man. With this concept of kingship in mind, the full significance of Paul's statements becomes clear. But this idea of the Christian life seems far removed from the actual lives most Christians live.

RIVAL SOVEREIGNTIES

Four regions are alluded to in Romans chapter 5.

"Death reigned from Adam to Moses" (v. 14)

"Sin hath reigned unto death" (v. 21)

"Even so might *grace* reign through righteousness" (v. 21)

"They . . . shall reign in life" (v. 17)

To use Paul's imagery, there are two eternally antagonistic dynasties endeavoring to capture and reign over the citadel of Mansoul—the dynasty of sin and death, and the dynasty of grace and righteousness. Between the two stands the Christian whose decision determines which dynasty shall have the ascendancy. Zoroastrianism sees the whole universe as a battleground between these two dynasties, between the god Ormuzd and the god Ahriman. That which settles a man's destiny is the side he chooses in the cosmic conflict.

We are left in no doubt of the Divine purpose and provision. "They shall reign in life." "Even so, might grace reign." God intends His children to live triumphant, not defeated lives. Paul himself testified, "But thanks be to God, for He always leads me in His triumphal train through union with Christ" (II Cor. 2:14, Williams). The picture is of a king who has returned from a triumphant campaign and is being honored by his emperor and nation.

There is a vast discrepancy between the life ideally depicted in the Scriptures and that actually lived by most Christians. Some enjoy lives of spiritual affluence, others live in spiritual penury, always on the bread line. Some believers exist, some live, a few reign. It is we ourselves who determine the level on which our lives are lived, whether in slavery to sin or reigning in righteousness.

ROYAL PRIVILEGES

The idea of royalty is normally associated with certain desirable characteristics whose spiritual counterparts should appear in the life of the Christian. In the reigning Queen of England, even though she does not exercise the absolute powers of the royalty of Paul's day, we both expect and find a *nobility of character*. Consciousness of her royal descent and strict self-discipline have produced in her a dignity and bearing which become one in her exalted position. We look in her for *charm of personality*, nor are we disappointed. To rich and poor alike she shows the same gracious interest and concern. On her royal tours, no matter how exacting the demands or how exhausted she has become, there is no loss of charm and winsomeness. Then, too, there is a *consciousness of authority* begotten by constant exercise of the prerogatives which her royal position confers on her. Those who come in contact with her are conscious of her authority and take no liberties. She suffers from *no limitation of wealth*. For her, to desire is to have. No matter what riches are displayed in clothing or jewels, there is always the impression of unlimited resources as yet untouched. She enjoys, theoretically at any rate, an *unfettered freedom*. The whole land is hers, and others enjoy its use only by grant from her. She can go where she will, do what she likes throughout her whole realm.

What a fascinating picture of Christian living this vivid picture portrays: nobility, charm, authority, wealth, freedom. Our God invites us to believe that these spiritual qualities and prerogatives may and should be enjoyed by every child of the King of kings. If we do not manifest and enjoy them, it is not because they are beyond our reach, but only because we are living below our privileges. God is always prodigal of His gifts. If it is love He bestows, it is "love that passeth knowledge." Or joy, it is "joy unspeakable and full of glory." Or peace, it is "peace that passeth all understanding." Our God is the God of the superlative.

Mrs. Hetty Green was a recluse who lived in a closely sealed apartment in an American city. She was fabulously wealthy, having inherited $20,000,000 of railway stock. On her death it was discovered that in place of an underskirt, she wore newspapers sewn together! In this way she was able to save some money but it could not be said that she was living up to either her privileges or her resources!

Must we not admit that we too live on a scale far below our spiritual resources? We are not always "more than conquerors." Instead of reigning over ourselves, our circumstances, our sins, we are frequently under their dominion. We wistfully read the categorical assurance, "Sin shall not have dominion over you," but have to confess with confusion of face, "O Lord our God, other lords besides thee have had dominion over us" (Isa. 26:13). The alluring promise of Romans 5:17 remains a tantalizing mirage. Instead of being robed in royal apparel, we are wearing our old newspapers. "I know full well that this is an experience into which all do not enter," wrote Dr. W. M. Clow. "It is a range of well-being and felicity to which some men dare not aspire and other men do not crave to attain. *All our lives are lived on a needlessly low level.*"

THE ROYAL SUBJECTS

Reigning implies subjects. What are they? The reign of sin and death is the reign of a power over a personality. The reign of grace and righteousness is a reign of a personality over a power. "*They* shall reign." The rights of royalty over powers which would impoverish and tyrannize have been bestowed on us.

Sin. "Sin shall not have dominion over you." If we are living under the dominion of sin it is either because we are ignorant of the way of deliverance or deep in our being we do not want to be delivered. It is not because full provision for liberation has not been made in the death and resurrection of Christ and the indwelling of the Holy Spirit. Because "death hath no more dominion over Him" says Paul, "sin shall not have dominion over you" (Rom. 6:9, 14). Besetting sin holds many of us in its vise-like grasp and throttles our spiritual life. But we can reign over every form of sin. No longer need our special besetment mar our spiritual experience.

Circumstances. We either reign over our circumstances or they reign over us. There is no middle path. We are their playthings or they are our subjects. In the closing verses of Romans 8, Paul lists the worst possible circumstances in which the believer could find himself—tribulation, distress, persecution, famine, nakedness, peril, sword—and then adds, "Nay in *all* these things we are more than conquerors *through him* that loved us" (Rom. 8:35, 37). No concessions need be made to the weakness of the flesh when the triumph of Christ is our triumph.

Frustration. This word has become very popular in the psychological jargon of our day, because it characterizes so many who, not having submitted to the lordship of Christ, have found life purposeless and frustrating. There need be no frustration to the person who has embraced the will of God as his rule of life. It was prophesied of Jesus before His birth and abundantly evidenced in His life, "I delight to do thy will, O my God" (Ps. 40:8). This does not sound like frustration. When life has as its supreme purpose the doing of God's will, that is a source of endless joy and delight.

Inadequacy. What is usually advanced as an excuse for low-level living and scanty spiritual service, may in reality prove a great blessing. "Blessed are the poor in spirit"— the inadequate—said our Lord. But inadequacy brings blessedness only when it throws us back on the limitless resources of Christ. Pleading our inadequacy does not please God, as Moses learned. When He calls to any task, the call carries with it the implication that all necessary enabling will be given. Paul's testimony was, "I can do all things through Christ which strengtheneth me."

Emotional States. No tyranny can be more despotic than that of our feelings and nothing more devastating to those with whom we live and work. In many homes there is a state of constant tension, if not violent discord because some member or members know nothing of reigning over their emotional states. They diffuse an "atmosphere" wherever they go. Other members of the family look covertly at them when they come down in the morning to discover in which way the wind is blowing, what kind of feeling is in the ascendancy. We should bear in mind that feelings are not responsible things. They are but the reflection of our inner state. If we ourselves are undisciplined, our feelings will be undisciplined too. If we are right at the center of our being in our relationship with the Lord, we will be right at the circumference as well. We should *live in the realm of the will,* not of the emotions. We become what we choose. Reigning is not an emotional state. It is the purposeful exercise of conscious prerogatives. God means that we should ascend the throne and reign over our feelings.

Fears. The writer to the Hebrews speaks of those who "through fear . . . were all their lifetime subject to bondage."

> Bound, who should be conquerors,
> Slaves, who should be free.

Fear frequently has a basis in reality, but more often it is something intangible, a nameless dread that grips and benumbs the spirit. Some people are afraid of everything. They fear people, the past, the future; they fear everything unknown; they fear undertaking responsibility and making decisions, and "fear hath torment" (I John 4:18). But it is gloriously possible for us to reign over all our fears, for "He hath said, I will never leave thee, nor forsake thee. So that we may boldly say, The Lord is my helper, and I will not fear." Note that two things are involved in reigning over fear—confidence in the assured companionship of God, and the fixed determination of the will, because He is our helper, that we will not fear. The ever-present God is there to reinforce the weak human will.

THE ROYAL RESOURCES

If the verse we are studying means anything, it means that there is no spiritual blessing which we can ever need or desire which God has not made available to us. Note the inventory of the resources at our disposal: "His more than sufficient grace," "the free gift of righteousness." We may give intellectual assent to the theological truth that God's grace is more than sufficient for our needs, and yet experimentally it may be absolutely untrue. The resources are available but they may be unappropriated.

It is to be noted that our "living like kings" and "reigning in life" are never apart from Christ. Paul makes this abundantly clear. "They shall reign in life *by one, Jesus Christ.*" Our reigning in life is the direct outcome of His reign in us. If He reigns in us, we reign in life. He has already made available to us the spoils of His victory but they await our appropriation.

"God . . . *hath blessed us* with all spiritual blessings . . . *in Christ*" (Eph. 1:3).

"He that spared not his own Son, but delivered him up for us all, how shall He not *with him* also freely give us all things?" (Rom. 8:32).

"All things are yours . . . and ye are Christ's; and Christ is God's" (I Cor. 3:21, 23).

These verses make it crystal clear that God has no favorites. There is no difference in bestowal between one Christian and another. There are no handicapped believers where royal resources are concerned. All may share alike. The only difference is in reception.

It may be asked, since these resources are available to all in Christ, why is there so little evidence of their possession in lives of Christians as a whole? Can the head be rich and the body poor? Yes, when the blood flow is restricted. Faith is the blood of the spiritual life and when faith is not functioning, spiritual penury is the inevitable result.

THE ROYAL SECRET

"They that *receive* . . . shall *reign*," Paul asserts. Receiving and reigning are Siamese twins. One cannot live separated from the other. What God has joined, man cannot put asunder. If some become spiritual giants while others remain spiritual pigmies, it is because some have been great receivers while others have allowed God's more than sufficient grace to remain unappropriated.

Appropriation lays hold of God's facts and turns them into factors of Christian experience. It claims God's promises, being "fully persuaded, that what he had promised, he was able also to perform." It staggers "not at the promise of God through unbelief." We each have the same spiritual resources to our credit as the greatest saint who ever lived. The degree in which we "live like kings" and "reign in life" will be the degree in which we draw on them and turn them into the currency of experience. In His matchless parable of the prodigal son, our Lord made it clear that the won-

derful father "divided unto *them* his living"—to the elder
brother equally with the younger son. And yet the former
complained, "Thou never gavest me a kid that I might make
merry with my friends." The difference was not in the bestowal but in the appropriation. The prodigal son at least
did his father the honor of receiving what he had been
given.

Our enjoyment of spiritual blessings is strictly limited to
our appropriation of them. We enjoy not what we long for,
or hope for, or even ask for, but only what we receive. We
can sigh for a reigning experience all our lives, but it becomes ours only when we appropriate the assurance of His
promise, "They that receive . . . *shall* reign," and only then.
Canaan was given to Israel by God but they did not enjoy
its blessings and benefits for many years—not until they personally appropriated it by walking over it. They could have
entered forty years sooner had they received and made their
own what God had already given them.

If we have a credit at the bank, there is no necessity to
implore the teller to give it to us. We only need to claim
what is ours by passing across a check. There are said to be
thirty thousand promises made to the child of God, but they
are of no more value to us than statements in the newspaper
if we do not personally appropriate them.

Towering above the City Hall in Philadelphia is a statue
of William Penn, the Quaker founder of the commonwealth
of Pennsylvania. He was on very good terms with the Indians and in recognition of his kindness they one day told
him that they would give him as much land as he could walk
around in a day. He took them at their word. Next morning he rose very early and walked all day long. It was late
at night when he returned and he was met by a group of
Indians with quizzical smiles on their faces. "Paleface has
had a very long walk today," they said. But they kept their
promise, and Penn received all the land which is now the
city of Philadelphia. Will God be less faithful to His promises?

It may be objected that the illustrations used are of tangible things, whereas spiritual blessings are intangible and the appropriation of them seems more difficult. But do we not appropriate intangible things constantly? Love may be lavished without stint but it is not enjoyed until it is believed and received. Forgiveness may be freely bestowed but it brings no release until it is believed and received. Our Lord enunciated an unalterable law of the spiritual life when He said, "According to your faith be it unto you." You will get only what you take.

The late Dr. F. B. Meyer recounted how he learned the royal secret of appropriation. He was addressing a large gathering of children who became increasingly unruly. He found his patience rapidly ebbing out and knew that he was about to lose his temper over which he had never fully reigned. He was ashamed of his failure but was unable to do anything about it. In his extremity he cried in his heart, "Thy patience, Lord!" Immediately it seemed as though a lump of the cooling patience of Christ dropped into his heart. All anger and annoyance completely died and he was able to bring the meeting to a blessed conclusion.

The experience was so striking, so decisive, and the deliverance so complete that he knew he had discovered a valuable secret. He testified that ever afterwards he used the same formula. He retained the words, "Thy . . . Lord!" and put between them whatever was his present need. Did he feel lonely? "Thy companionship, Lord!" Did fear grip? "Thy serenity, Lord!" Did impurity tempt? "Thy purity, Lord!" Was he feeling critical of others? "Thy love, Lord!" God had given him "all things that pertain unto life and godliness," and he appropriated them just as the need arose. He found Christ to be the complement of his every need. He proved, as will we, that there is a world of difference between the faith that asks and the faith that appropriates. Only those who receive, reign in life.

PART III

THE SPIRIT—THE BREATH OF GOD

"There came a sound as of a rushing mighty wind [breath]" Acts 2:2

READING: John 20:19—23; Acts 2:1-4

STUCK BETWEEN EASTER AND PENTECOST." This arresting diagnosis of the spiritual condition of many Christians is worthy of careful thought and personal application. It is possible to rejoice in the fact that Christ is risen without passing on to experience the enduement with power promised by the risen Christ, of which Pentecost was the prototype. Why the vast discrepancy between the spiritual power wielded by the early church and that exercised by the church of our day? The simple explanation is that we cannot have the fruits without the roots. The early church achievement was the outcome of the early church enduement. Scripture makes it satisfyingly clear that this unction and its replenishment are as available to the Christian of today as on the Day of Pentecost.

Pentecost was the necessary complement of Calvary. Like an ellipse, the Christian faith and Christian experience revolve around these twin centers. Without Pentecost, Calvary would have failed of its purpose and been ineffectual to redeem a lost world. It would have been like perfecting a costly machine and neglecting to provide the motive power. The great facts on which redemption is based, our Lord's virgin birth, virtuous life, vicarious death and victorious resurrection, had been completed for more than forty days, and yet nothing had happened—until the Day of Pentecost. Only then did the machinery of redemption swing into motion.

132

The Day of Pentecost witnessed the coalescing of the sovereign purpose of God and the spiritual preparation of the men to whom He was entrusting its fulfillment. The exact timing of the descent of the Spirit had been indicated centuries earlier. The feast of Pentecost was to be celebrated fifty days after the feast of Passover (Lev. 23). The Day of Pentecost must follow fifty days after "Christ our passover" was sacrificed for us. And it did, with all its blessed accompaniments.

Two of the great revivalists of a past generation were Jonathan Edwards and Charles G. Finney. Edwards viewed revival as a sovereign act of God which could in no way be influenced by man's preparations or endeavors. Finney, on the contrary, maintained that God was always ready to bestow revival, and that man could have it whenever he was ready to pay the price in heart preparation. The Day of Pentecost demonstrated that both were right and both were wrong. The Holy Spirit descended only "when the day of Pentecost was *fully* come" (Acts 2:1). No amount of self-emptying or heart preparation on the disciples' part would have induced His descent on any other day. But this sovereign act of God coincided with deep humbling and self-abasement on their part. The Spirit would not have come upon men and women in whose hearts there had been no prior preparation. The ten days of waiting and prayer had produced an intolerable craving for the fulfillment of "the promise of the Father" (Luke 24:49). At Pentecost God's sovereign purpose and man's essential preparation came to maturity, and immediately there followed a spontaneous Divine intervention. "There came . . . from heaven" three supernatural phenomena.

"And suddenly there came a sound from heaven as of a rushing mighty wind, and it filled all the house where they were sitting" (Acts 2:2). This was a corporate experience, signifying the mysterious renewing and purifying of the Spirit in the Church.

"And there appeared unto them cloven tongues like as of

fire, and it sat upon each of them" (Acts 2:3). This was an individual experience, symbolizing the Spirit's melting, warming, purging ministry.

"They were all filled with the Holy Ghost, and began to speak with other tongues, as the Spirit gave them utterance. . . . Now when this was noised abroad, the multitude . . . were confounded, because that every man heard them speak in his own language" (Acts 2:4, 6).

This was the outcome of Spirit-empowered witness of men and women with tongues aflame as they spoke of the wonderful works of God—a reversal of Babel. Then, they were confounded because one language became many. Now, they are confounded because many languages became one.

While there was a dispensational and historical side to Pentecost, it had also personal and practical implications for the early disciples and for us who have believed on Christ through their word (John 17:20). They themselves knew that something momentous had happened in them. Instead of hiding behind closed doors "for fear of the Jews" (John 20:19), "they spake the word with boldness" and "ate their bread with gladness . . . praising God, and having favour with all the people" (Acts 2:46, 47).

The multitudes assembled in Jerusalem knew that something inexplicable had happened to the disciples. In their endeavors to explain this miraculous change, the mockers said, "These men are full of new wine." They were nearer the truth than they suspected, and yet infinitely removed from it. Ready as ever with his answer, Peter replied in effect, "Yes, they are intoxicated, but not from an earthly source. Their inebriation springs from another Spirit" (Acts 2:14-18). They were intoxicated, not with the Devil's stimulant, but with the Divine Stimulus. Men usually resort to stimulants because they are conscious of inadequacy and inability to cope with the exigencies of life. They must have some external stimulus. God, who knows the full extent of human inadequacy, has made adequate provision for this universal need. Paul refers to it in his antithetical exhortation, "Be not drunk with wine, wherein is excess; but be filled with the Spirit" (Eph. 5:18). He Himself is the Divine Stimulus.

The extent of the transformation the coming of the Holy Spirit effected in the waiting disciples was staggering. The Risen Christ became vividly real to them. They preached as though He was at their very elbow. They received entirely new insight into the significance of familiar Old Testament Scriptures. Linking passage with passage, Peter was able to say with assurance, "This is that which was spoken by the prophet" (Acts 2:16). Their speech became authoritative and incisive and their Spirit-given words produced deep conviction (Acts 2:37). They left saving impressions on the minds of their hearers, and became utterly fearless in their witness (Acts 4:31).

One of the most significant changes in their attitude was their willingness to submerge themselves in the interests of the progress of the Gospel. Hitherto there had been constant strife for precedence among them. Now they are a self-forgetful team with one objective—to preach Christ. Dr. A. B. Simpson made a challenging statement in this connection: "Not many rivers flow into the sea. Most rivers run into other rivers. The best workers are not those who demand a separate sphere of influence and prestige for themselves, but are content to empty their streams of blessing into other rivers."

Such was the transformation wrought in the early Christians by the advent of the Holy Spirit. How can a comparable experience of His transforming power take place in our lives? The first message of the Risen Lord to His disciples throws light on this very question of personal participation in the blessing and benefits of the Holy Spirit's ministry:

> Then the same day at evening, being the first day
> of the week, when the doors were shut where the dis-
> ciples were assembled for fear of the Jews, came Jesus
> and stood in the midst, and saith unto them, Peace be

unto you. And when he had so said, he showed unto
them his hands and his side. Then were the disciples
glad, when they saw the Lord. Then said Jesus to them
again, Peace be unto you: as my Father hath sent me,
even so send I you. And when he had said this, He
breathed on them, and saith unto them, Receive ye
the Holy Ghost (John 20:19-22).

In order that we may understand the significance of our
Lord's symbolical act of breathing on—or better into—the
disciples, we should note that the word "Spirit" is derived
from the Latin *spiritus*—breath. We "inspire" when we
breathe in and "expire" when we breathe out. The Greek
word for the Spirit, *pneuma*, also means wind or breath.
The Hebrew word for Spirit, *ruach*, has the same significance. Job, adopting the Hebrew poetic device of the repetition of ideas said, "The Spirit of God hath made me, and
the breath of the Almighty hath given me life" (33:4), thus
identifying "the breath of the Almighty" with "the Spirit of
God," In so doing he used a figure of speech which is con-
sistently used of Him throughout Scripture. He is so called
because He is the direct emanation of God, the manifestation
of His very presence.

It was the Breath of God which produced order out of
chaos in the beginning (Gen. 1:2). Man became a living
soul by God breathing into his nostrils the breath of life
(Gen. 2:7). Ezekiel witnessed lifeless corpses become a
living army when in obedience to the Divine command he
prayed, "Come from the four winds, O breath, and breathe
upon these slain, that they may live" (37:9).

With this in mind, let us consider the symbolic act of
Christ, in which He graphically revealed to His disciples the
source of their power. First there was the twice repeated
bestowal of peace (John 20:19, 21). Next the Great Commission: "As my Father hath sent me, even so send I you"
(20:21). Then the imparting of the Spirit. "He breathed on
[into] them, and saith unto them, Receive ye the Holy
Ghost" (v. 22), without whose aid they would be powerless

to execute His commission. This was a miniature anticipation of the full-scale bestowal of the Spirit at Pentecost, and teaches a valuable lesson. It was as though He was saying, "All you have to do is to breathe in, to take the Holy Spirit I impart to you now. He is the power to enable you to fulfil My commission."

This graphic outbreathing and inbreathing illustrates the method of reception of the Spirit. The disciples breathed in what Christ breathed out. Could any illustration be more simple? On the Day of Pentecost God breathed out—"there came from heaven the sound as of a rushing mighty wind [breath]." They breathed in, and "they were all filled with the Holy Ghost." Breathing in is simply the equivalent of receiving. When we breathe in, the same life-giving qualities as are in the atmosphere are in us. When we breathe in or receive the Holy Spirit, that which is peculiar to Him becomes peculiar to us, just as when we place iron in the fire, the fire enters the iron and the iron partakes of the properties peculiar to the fire.

It is a familiar law that nature abhors a vacuum. In breathing we create a vacuum by breathing out and fill the vacuum by breathing in. If we are to know either an initial or a renewed experience of the filling of the Spirit, there must first be the abandoning of every other dependence, a breathing out, and then the appropriating of His sufficiency and power as our own, a breathing in.

Dr. J. Wilbur Chapman, noted American evangelist who with Charles Alexander exercised a mighty evangelistic ministry around the world, was at one time deeply concerned at the lack of fruitfulness in his ministry. "What is the matter with me?" he inquired of Dr. F. B. Meyer. "So many times I fail, so many times I am powerless. What is the reason?" "Have you ever tried breathing out three times without breathing in once?" was the quiet rejoinder. Dr. Chapman needed no further explanation.

It might be objected that in this age, which is the dispensation of the Holy Spirit, there is no need for the believer to receive the Holy Spirit since, as Paul says, "If any man have not the Spirit of Christ, he is none of his" (Rom. 8:9). This is, of course, true but not every believer *knows* that he has the Spirit or knows the Spirit whom he has (John 14:17). When Paul met the twelve disciples at Ephesus, he asked, "Did ye receive the Holy Spirit when ye believed? And they said unto him, Nay, we did not so much as hear whether the Holy Spirit was given" (Acts 19:2, A.S.V.). If they were true believers they were indwelt by the Holy Spirit, but their ignorance of the fact deprived them of the benefits of much of His ministry in their lives. It was only with the advent of Paul that they knew anything of His power. Was it not this very possibility of ignorance which caused Paul to write to the Corinthian Christians, "Know ye not that ye are the temple of God, and that the Spirit of God dwelleth in you?" (I Cor. 3:16). In its full sense "receiving" involves conscious volition. Possession and conscious reception do not always go together.

There is not much benefit to me in having a check for $1,000 in my pocket if I do not know it is there; or if while knowing it is there I have no conception of its value. I have received it in the sense that I possess the piece of paper. But in actuality I have not received it until I present it at the bank and receive its value in cash.

If this be true, it is our part to breathe out—to exhale from our lives all that is impure and unworthy, and then to breathe in—to consciously appropriate the Holy Spirit for ourselves in His absolute sufficiency. He has been sent to be the Saviour's Representative to guide, control, empower. When we receive Him in this capacity, He who dwelt in us unconsciously, is now able to exercise His gracious ministry with our full knowledge and consent.

> Breathe on me, Breath of God,
>   Fill me with life anew,
> That I may love what Thou dost love,
>   And do what Thou wouldst do.

THE TRANSFORMING POWER OF
THE SPIRIT

"But we all, with open face beholding as in a glass the glory of the Lord, are changed into the same image from glory to glory, even as by the Spirit of the Lord"
(II Corinthians 3:18)

READING: II Corinthians 3:1-18

How MAY WE ACQUIRE likeness to Christ?" This verse provides a satisfying answer to this wistful question of many hearts. There is not only one answer to that question, for there are many varieties of Christian experience, and the fullness of blessing is not experienced by all in the same manner or through the same aspect of truth. But this paragraph sets out in unmistakable terms one of the great secrets of conformity to the image of Christ.

The context of this alluring possibility draws a striking contrast between the old covenant of law and the new covenant of grace—the passing glory of the one, the surpassing splendor of the other—between Moses with face veiled, and the believer with veil removed. The requirement of the old covenant was that man, by his own unaided effort, should live up to the exacting standard of God's holiness in the decalogue, a requirement which led only to deep despair. The supreme revelation of the new covenant was that transformation of character into the likeness of Christ comes not by painful striving, but by beholding and believing and the operation of the Holy Spirit in the heart of the believer. The old covenant which came by Moses was a ministration of death and condemnation, but the new covenant which was

139

ushered in by the death of Christ was a ministration of righteousness and life (vv. 7, 8). The aspiration of Moses under the old covenant was expressed in his request, "I beseech thee, show me thy glory." The realization of this aspiration in the new covenant is seen in the text, "We all, with unveiled face, beholding . . . the glory of the Lord are changed into the same image."

AN OBJECTIVE VISION

"We all with open [unveiled] face beholding as in a glass the glory of the Lord." Transformation of character begins not with subjective introspection, but with an objective vision of the glory of the Lord and the Lord of glory. It is "Christ Jesus, who of God is made unto us sanctification [holiness]" (I Cor. 1:30). And where may this captivating vision be seen? Not in illuminated heavens but in the written Word—the mirror which reveals His perfect manhood, His flawless character, His unique Person and His mediatorial work. Concerning the Word of God, Jesus said, "Search the scriptures . . . they are they which testify of me" (John 5:39). Paul asserts that "the light of the knowledge of the glory of God" may be seen "in the face of Jesus Christ" (II Cor. 4:6). But where can that face be authentically seen? Not on a painter's canvas, for the most beautiful painting is only the projection of the artist's conception of Christ. It can be seen only in the records of His inspired biographers who under the guidance of the Holy Spirit have given us with meticulous accuracy a full-length portrait of Him.

The Jews saw the Face, but they missed the glory because a veil lay over their minds, a veil of prejudice and hatred and unbelief far more impenetrable than the veil which concealed Moses' radiant face (v. 7). But, says Paul, through Christ this veil is taken away (v. 14). And now "we all"— not a select group of especially holy people—"with unveiled face" may gaze at His glory. The glory here referred to is, of course, the moral glory of Christ, His excellences of character and conduct, which shine out everywhere in the Scriptures.

A SUBJECTIVE TRANSFORMATION

"Are being changed into the same image." This objective vision has a subjective purpose, that we might be changed into His likeness. God is not satisfied with us as we are. Nor are we satisfied with ourselves as we are if we really know ourselves. The Son of Man was to the Father such an object of delight, He so perfectly fulfilled all His purposes and conformed to His standard, that He plans for all His children to be "changed" or, as the word is, "transfigured" into His likeness. When our Lord was transfigured before His disciples, for a moment He drew aside the veil of flesh which concealed His innate and essential glory and allowed the three on the mount to briefly glimpse it. "We beheld His glory, the glory as of the only begotten of the Father," said John several decades later. "We were eyewitnesses of His majesty," said Peter, another of the favored three on the mount of transfiguration. We have no such inherent and essential glory. The Divine purpose for us is not mere external imitation but internal transformation. And the transformation will not be transient and evanescent. We shall not lose the glory as did Moses. "The children of Israel could not steadfastly behold the face of Moses for the glory of his countenance; which glory was to be done away" (v. 7). Ours is to be glory retained and transmitted. "For if that which is done away was glorious, much more *that which remaineth* is glorious" (v. 11).

And the method of transformation? "Beholding." Not a despairing struggle against that which captivates, but a steady, concentrated gazing on Christ and a confident relying on the Holy Spirit to effect the change.

The word used here for "beholding" may with equal propriety be rendered either "beholding" or "reflecting." As we behold His glory, we are changed into His likeness. As we are changed, we reflect as in a mirror the image into which we are transformed. Reflecting is the inevitable result of beholding.

It is a law of life that we become like those we constantly gaze at. The eye exercises a great influence on life and character. The education of a child is conducted largely through the eye. He is molded by the manners and habits of those he constantly sees. This is the explanation of the powerful influence of the movies on young people. They become like that on which they gaze. Look on the streets of a large city and you will see counterparts of famous actresses. Their fans copy them in dress, in speech, in behavior. We become like those we admire. Alexander the Great studied Homer's *Iliad* and as a result he went out to conquer the world. William Cowper, the celebrated poet, when a young and sensitive boy, read a treatise in favor of suicide. Who can doubt that when, later in life, he attempted to destroy himself, it was the influence of the book which had gripped him in earlier days. In the spiritual realm, how many famous preachers have numerous smaller editions of themselves among their admirers!

On one occasion the writer was holidaying at an isolated spot. When the Lord's Day came, the only church service of any kind was conducted by a Salvation Army soldier, an illiterate farmer. His text was the one at the head of this chapter. He was not eloquent. He did not evidence deep learning. Some of his exegesis was questionable. But his reiteration of his text etched four words indelibly on the mind—"*beholding, we are changed.*" His radiant face and obvious joy in the Lord were exemplification of the truth of his claim. A glance of faith may save, but it is the gaze of faith which sanctifies, said Robert Murray McCheyne. A hurried glance at Christ snatched after lying abed too late will never effect a radical transformation of character.

Dr. A. B. Simpson sees us here as the photography of God, the Holy Spirit developing and perfecting Him in the midst of our lives. If the image is to be perfect, the sitter must be in focus. The veil must be removed. The sitter must remain quite still with steadfast gaze since it is a time exposure. After the image has been transferred to the sensitive film in

the moment of exposure, there follows the process by which
the acids etch away all that conceals the likeness of the subject. This is the ministry of the Holy Spirit who, as we yield
to His influence, removes all that is unlike Christ and imparts
to us His own perfections.

But we are also to *reflect* the glory of the Lord as Moses
did after his forty days' sojourn in the mount in the presence
of the glory of God. When we behold the glory of Christ in
the mirror of Scripture His glory shines upon us and into us,
and then is reflected by us. With Moses it was a transient
and fading reflection of the glory, but it need not be so with
us. It should be our constant aim to ensure that we are an
accurate reflection of Christ to the world of men around us.
It is very possible for His image in us to be distorted and
blurred in the course of transmission, as our own image has
been in a fun-fair mirror. Since unbelieving men can know
Christ only by what they see of Him in us, how important
that we do not misrepresent Him, that we do not display our
own carnal attitudes instead of His moral beauty and glory.
What they see of Christ reflected in us should turn their
antagonism and indifference into wistfulness and faith.

A PROGRESSIVE EXPERIENCE

"We are being changed into His likeness from one degree
of glory to another." Translators render this sentence differ-
ently, but in them all there is the idea of progression.
"Through successive stages of glory," "in ever increasing
splendor," "from a mere reflected to an inherent glory," "from
one degree of radiant holiness unto another." One thing is
clear. It is not the purpose of God that our Christian experience should be static. There lie ahead of us endless
possibilities of growth into the likeness of Christ. These
words clearly show that Christlikeness in all its fullness is not
the result merely of some moment of high and holy exaltation, but that it is a progressive experience. The inward
change produced in us by the Holy Spirit is to be daily

transforming us more nearly to the image of our Lord. We are transfigured by the renewing of our minds.

The Transforming Agent

"Even as by the Lord the Spirit." "The Lord the Spirit," as it is in the original, is an unusual phrase and poses a theological problem. William Barclay comments: "Paul seems to identify the Risen Lord and the Holy Spirit. We must remember that Paul was not writing theology; he was setting down experience. And it is the experience of the Christian life that the work of the Spirit and the work of the Risen Lord are one and the same. The strength, the light, the guidance we receive come alike from the Spirit and from the Risen Lord. It does not matter how we express it so long as we experience it."

We need to see in this transformation our responsibility and the Holy Spirit's ministry. The change into the likeness of Christ is not automatic. It involves moral endeavor and activity. We are not only to "let go and let God," we are also to "put off" and "put on" certain things, and this involves definite activity of the renewed will. It is not the inevitable result of passive daydreaming about Christ. Our part is to "behold the glory of the Lord" in active, expectant faith. The Spirit then exercises His prerogative of revealing the glory of Christ and reproducing that likeness in ever increasing splendor. We behold Him, but we trust and expect the Holy Spirit to change us into Christ's likeness. The transforming work is entirely His as He ministers and imparts to us all the values and virtues of the Person and work of Christ. We behold in silent adoring contemplation; He works into the fabric of our lives what we see in Jesus.

In achieving this, the Spirit exercises both a negative and a positive ministry. First, *He reveals to us the things in our life and character which are unlike Christ,* and therefore must go. Everything alien to the perfection of Christ must be "put off." This revealing ministry is not pleasant, indeed it can be devastating, for despite our protestations of unworthiness we are all greatly biased in our own favor. We do not enjoy others evaluating us as we profess to evaluate ourselves. But if we sincerely desire to be transformed, we will be willing to part with everything that mars Christ's image in us. God cannot "put off" these manifestations of unlikeness to Christ. It is something which we alone can do, and must do. Paul indicates elsewhere things which must be put off if we are to be assimilated into Christ. "Anger, wrath, malice, blasphemy, filthy communication out of your mouth. Lie not one to another" (Col. 3: 8-9).

But the Spirit not only reveals what must be discarded. He enables us to do it. "If ye *through the Spirit* do mortify the deeds of the body, ye shall live," were Paul's bracing words (Rom. 8:13). We are not left to our own unaided efforts as were those who lived under the old covenant. We have a mighty Paraclete whose supreme delight it is to aid us to the limit when our hearts are set on becoming like Christ in character and conduct.

Then *the Holy Spirit reveals the graces and blessings which should and could be ours,* and enables us to appropriate them. One of the tragedies of many Christian lives is the poverty of their experience when contrasted with the vastness of their unclaimed privileges. "Blessed be the God and Father of our Lord Jesus Christ," wrote Paul, "who *hath* blessed us with *all* spiritual blessings . . . in Christ." "*All things* are yours." "According as his divine power *hath given* unto us *all things* that pertain unto life and godliness." There is no grace which we behold in the character of our Lord which may not be ours in increasing measure as we look to the Spirit to produce it in us.

"Beholding . . . we are changed."

THE PURGING FIRE OF THE SPIRIT

"Then the fire of the Lord fell" (I Kings 18:38)

READING: I Kings 18:1-40

THIS STORY is one of the most dramatic in the Old Testament. Everything about it is vivid and colorful. The characters are spectacular, the issues tremendous, the outcome glorious.

Elijah, the lone prophet of Jehovah, was one of the most remarkable characters of Israel's history. He appears suddenly as the prophet of the crisis, the champion of Divine rights. He disappears as suddenly to the accompaniment of a chariot of fire and a whirlwind. The New Testament has more to say of him than of any prophet. Stepping out of the unknown, his first public act was to lock the heavens by his prayers so that no rain fell for three and a half years—in this instance a judgment on an idolatrous nation.

Though we have no record of his early life, there had undoubtedly been a private preparation for so powerful a public ministry. Such a career as his could only be the outcome of a personal encounter with God. In secret he had received his prophetic call. By secret tests he had so come to know God as to be absolutely sure of Him. Through secret fellowship with God he had been completely delivered from the fear of man. Physically, he was a sun-tanned sheik of rugged and austere appearance. Morally, he was a man of courage, faith and zeal.

Character is revealed in crises, and the secret of Elijah's life is epitomized in these words: "Lord God of Abraham, Isaac and of Israel, let it be known this day that thou art

God in Israel, and that I am thy servant, and that I have done all these things at thy word" (v. 36). The true man is seen in the place of prayer. Three facts emerge:

He had a consuming passion for the glory of God. "Let it be known that thou art God." This came first in his thoughts. His soul was filled with a holy jealousy for God's glory.

He was content to be the slave of Jehovah. "Let it be known that I am thy servant." He acknowledged God's absolute ownership.

He was implicitly obedient to the Divine commands. "I have done all these things at thy word."

The gathering of Israel (v. 19) was not the work of a moment. Judging by the outcome, it is not difficult to believe that Elijah spent much time in waiting on God and receiving from Him the plan of campaign. Such sublime confidence in God as he displayed could only be the outcome of prolonged communion with God. Elijah knew his God.

Elijah's dramatic challenge grew out of his deep concern over the apostasy of the nation. On the throne was the weakest and wickedest king Israel had known. Even before his marriage it is recorded that "Ahab did evil in the sight of the Lord above all that were before him." To this he added another base distinction. "And as if it had been a light thing for him to walk in the sins of Jeroboam, he took to wife Jezebel . . . and went and served Baal, and worshiped him. And Ahab did more to provoke the Lord God of Israel to anger than all the kings of Israel that were before him" (16: 30-33). Instead of Jehovah, Baal enjoyed pride of place in Israel's worship. It was at this juncture when true religion and morality had almost disappeared that Elijah dramatically walked on to the stage of Israel's history.

THE CHALLENGE OF THE FIRE

"The God that answereth by fire." There could be no compromise between the worship of Jehovah and the worship of Baal. The two contrasting systems of religion could not live together in peaceful co-existence. It is the man of God who precipitates the crisis. God always has His man to match the hour. He prepares him in secret and then manifests him in the hour of crisis. God is never without His witness. There is always a Luther or a Calvin, a Wesley or a Whitefield, a Moody or a Torrey or a Graham.

The grandeur of Elijah's character is nowhere more strikingly apparent than in the drama on Carmel. True, he was "a man of like passions" with us, but he was also a man of unlike courage and faith. Like Martin Luther, the lonely prophet fearlessly faced the assembled religious might of the nation. In the language of his day he proclaimed, "Here I stand, I can do no other." He threw down the gauntlet and challenged the false gods to a test of strength with his God. The test was eminently fair. Since Baal was the god of fire, let the test be his own element. "The god that answereth by fire, let him be God," was Elijah's reasonable suggestion. No objection could be raised. The issues were crystal clear. "If Jehovah be God, follow Him, but if Baal, then follow him." The crisis hour had come, and they must take one turning or the other.

THE SIGNIFICANCE OF THE FIRE

"The Lord descended in fire." The significance of the test by fire was not lost on the people of Israel. They could all recall occasions in their national history when God had answered by fire, and knew that the fire was the manifestation of the presence of God.

God manifested His presence to Moses in the burning bush. "Behold, the bush *burned with fire,* and the bush was not consumed. And God called unto him out of the midst of the bush" (Exod. 3:2, 4). The presence of God on Mount Sinai was evidenced by fire. "And Mount Sinai was altogether on a smoke *because the Lord descended on it in fire*" (Exod. 19:18). The presence of God in the midst of His people was symbolized by the fire which hovered over the Tabernacle by night. "And the glory of the Lord filled the tabernacle . . . and *fire was on it* by night, in the sight of all the house of Israel" (Exod. 40: 35, 38). There was a similar manifestation of the Divine presence at the dedication of the temple. "Now when Solomon had made an end of praying, *the fire came down from heaven* ... and the glory of the Lord filled the house" (II Chron. 7:1). The presence of the fire was proof of the presence of God.

Such was the significance of the symbol of fire in Old Testament times. But what is its meaning for us today? In the New Testament it is symbolic of the presence and energy of the Holy Spirit. Announcing the ministry of the Messiah, John the Baptist said, "He shall baptize you with the Holy Ghost, and *with fire*" (Matt. 3:11). His prophecy was fulfilled. On the Day of Pentecost when the Holy Spirit came with power upon the assembled disciples, the chosen symbol was prominent. "There appeared unto them cloven tongues *like as of fire*, and it sat upon each of them" (Acts 2:3). There is therefore justification for the view that the symbolism of fire in its present-day application is the presence and power of the Holy Spirit.

In Elijah's day the holy fire had disappeared from the altars of Jehovah; and false fire was burning on the altars of Baal. The glory had departed, and no man could rekindle the sacred flame. When Nadab and Abihu "offered strange fire before the Lord," they died, for there can be no substitute for the true fire of God.

In our day, the greatest lack in the life of the individual Christian and of the Church is the fire of God, the manifested presence and mighty working of the Holy Spirit. There is little about us that cannot be explained on the level of the natural. Our lives are not fire-touched. There is no holy conflagration in our churches to which people are irresistibly drawn as a moth to a flame. It is the absence of the fire of God which accounts for the insignificant impact the Church is making on a lost world. It never had better organization, a more scholarly ministry, greater resources of men and means, more skillful techniques. And yet never did it make a smaller contribution to solving the problems of a distraught

world. Our prayer should be, "Lord, send the fire." What
else can meet the need of the hour?

THE FALLING OF THE FIRE

"Then the fire of the Lord fell." The falling of the fire was
the crux and climax of the Carmel drama. All else had been
preparatory to this moment. Important spiritual lessons can
be learned from what preceded it. If we can discover the
fundamental factors, we will discover the source of spiritual
revival. "Then the fire . . . fell." When?

The fire fell *at a time of national apostasy.* Jehovah worship was at its lowest ebb and Baal worship had captured the
field. Spiritual darkness enveloped the whole land. God
does not limit the bestowal of His blessings to times when
conditions are most propitious. It is when the darkness is
deepest that the light is most needed, and no one will be
disposed to minimize the darkness of the hour in which we
live. No vivid imagination is required to see a real parallel
with conditions in our day. Satanic forces are abroad. The
church exerts little influence on the nation, although there
are still the seven thousand who have not bowed the knee
to Baal.

The fire fell *when Elijah obeyed God without hesitation.*
Earlier God had said to him, "Hide thyself." "So he went and
did according unto the word of the Lord." (I Kings 17:
3, 5). Now comes the unequivocal command, "Go, show thyself unto Ahab and I will send rain upon the earth" (18:1).
It is not difficult to appreciate how little Elijah wished to
meet Ahab, his implacable enemy. For three years the vin-
dictive Ahab had been seeking his life. He could not forget
that it was Elijah's prayer that had closed the heavens and
smitten the land with drought. But before the drought could
be relieved, Elijah must obey the word of the Lord.

His obedience was just as prompt as when he was told to
hide himself. "And Elijah went to show himself unto Ahab"
(18:2). The falling of the fire and the coming of the rain
were the direct result of Elijah's obedience to facing Ahab,

the personification of moral and spiritual evil. We will seek in vain the falling of the fire of God if there is some reserved area in our lives concerning which we refuse to obey God. If He is pressing on us the necessity of some act of obedience, restitution, apology or witness, we refuse to obey at our own cost. He cannot move in blessing until there has been obedience.

The fire fell *after the ruined altar had been repaired*. "He repaired the altar of the Lord that was broken down" (v. 30). The ruined altar spoke volumes. An altar is a symbol of worship. Carmel, it would appear, had been a secret meeting place for the people of God, but the altar had fallen into disuse and disrepair, the worship of Jehovah had ceased. Before the fire can fall, the altar must be rebuilt. Elijah took the twelve stones—he did not recognize the division between the northern and southern kingdoms—and rebuilt the altar. His objective was a reunited nation with the manifested presence of God among them. The fire of God falls when there is spiritual unity among God's people. If there is some altar in our lives which has fallen into disrepair, the fire will not fall until it is re-erected. What does the altar pre-eminently typify? Did Christ not offer Himself on the altar of the Cross? Only when the Cross in its full significance is restored to its central place will the fire of the Lord fall.

The fire fell *when the whole offering was placed on the altar*. "He . . . cut the bullock in pieces, and laid him on the wood" (v. 33). The fire of God never falls on an empty altar. The dismembering of the sacrifice is not without its spiritual significance. It is easy in a moment of exaltation and high resolve to place the whole life on the altar, but it is in the members of the body that the consecration has to be lived out, as F. R. Havergal so beautifully says in her consecration hymn. It begins with "Take my life," but it proceeds, "Take my hands . . . my feet . . . my voice . . . my love." It is not one great initial dedication only, but continuing acts of surrender. God will not be satisfied with a partial surrender. Ananias and Sapphira presented part to God, pretending it to be all, but at what tragic cost to themselves. Abraham was called upon by God to surrender to God the worst thing in his life and the best thing in his life. He had to surrender Ishmael, son of his carnal unbelief and send him away from his paternal tent into the wilderness. He had to place on the altar Isaac, son of his sublime faith, and lift the sacrificial knife. Then the fire of the Lord fell on Abraham and there came the Divine response, "In thy seed shall all the nations of the earth be blessed; because thou hast obeyed my voice." The last piece of the sacrifice had been placed on the altar. We cannot deceive God. He knows when the altar is full and His response will not tarry. When Elijah placed the last piece of the sacrifice on the altar, there was the flash of flame.

The fire fell *after the counterfeit had been excluded*. "Fill four barrels of water, and pour it on the burnt sacrifice, and on the wood . . . and the water ran round about the altar" (vv. 33, 35). Elijah allowed no room for false fire. Three times in his challenge to the prophets of Baal he stipulated, "Put no fire under." There was to be no trickery, no insertion of a secret spark. But he was equally strict with himself. Every precaution was taken against deception. He wished it to be clear that the fire which fell on his altar was kindled in Heaven. "Come near unto me," he invited the people. He had nothing to fear from their scrutiny. So sure was he of his God that he heaped difficulties in the way. The water would soon have quenched any hidden spark. His was the faith that laughs at impossibilities. Not many have a buoyant faith like this. Our inclination would be to help God out by pouring gasoline on the sacrifice for easier ignition! Elijah wished it to be evident that he had no alternative but God. It is for us, too, to guard against counterfeit, the substitution of the psychic for the spiritual, or mass hypnotism for the power of the Holy Spirit.

The fire fell *after Elijah had prayed the prayer of faith*. Elijah said, "Lord . . . let it be known this day that thou art God in Israel, and that I am thy servant, and that I have done all these things at thy word. Hear me, O Lord, hear

ne, that this people may know that thou art the Lord God"
vv. 36, 37).

What a contrast this, to the frenzied yelling of the priests
f Baal as they leaped on their altar, calling on their un-
esponsive god and cutting themselves with lances till the
lood gushed out! But no fire from Heaven fell in answer to
heir frantic cries. Before offering the prayer of faith Elijah
ad laughed the laugh of faith. The silence of Heaven proved
he futility of their claims for Baal. So sure was he of the
esponse of Jehovah that with withering sarcasm he taunted
hem and their god. "Cry aloud; for he is a god; either he is
alking, or he is pursuing, or he is in a journey, or peradven-
ure he sleepeth and must be awaked" (v. 27). In this utter-
nce Elijah had so committed both himself and his God that
God could not let His servant down. Such a display of con-
idence was well-pleasing to God. "The immortal test of
Elijah, made in the presence of an apostate king, and in the
ace of a backslidden nation and an idolatrous priesthood on
Mount Carmel, is a sublime exhibition of faith and prayer,"
vrote E. M. Bounds.

No sooner had this simple prayer for the vindication of
God and His servant been offered than there was a flash from
Heaven. "*Then* the fire of the Lord fell." The fire did not fall
n stages. The prayer of faith was immediately followed by
the fire from Heaven. Sacrifice, wood, stones, water, alike
offered no resistance to the heavenly flame. Elijah's heart's
desire was realized. The supremacy of Jehovah was established. The presence and power of the true God was once
again manifest among His people. The honor of both God
and His servant was vindicated. The pretensions of the Baal
worshipers were demolished. When our prayers are motivated by the desire "that the Father may be glorified in the
Son," we too shall see the fire fall.

THE ACHIEVEMENT OF THE FIRE

The falling of the fire *brought all Israel on their faces.*
"And when all the people saw it, they fell on their faces: and

they said, the Lord, he is the God; the Lord, he is the God" (v. 39). The testimony of the man of God was vindicated by fire from the God who Himself is a consuming fire. They could not deny the evidence of their eyes. A godless world will begin to pay attention to our witness when they see the fire of God in our midst, the manifestation of the presence and power of the Holy Spirit at work among us.

The falling of the fire *resulted in the death of the false prophets.* Elijah's first act was to command Israel to bring with their own hands the priests of Baal to be killed. All rivals to the true God must be overthrown. The falling of the true fire automatically involved the removal of the false fire from the altars of Baal. Only the fire from Heaven gave Elijah the moral authority for such a purging as this.

The falling of the fire *accomplished patent impossibilities.* Whoever heard of stones being consumed? And yet it was done. At Pentecost the fire of God accomplished the impossible in the lives of the apostles. Cowardice was burnt up and gave place to courage, doubt to faith, self-seeking to selflessness and a passion for the glory of Christ. Qualities of character which previously were conspicuous by their absence now flourished.

After the Great Plague in London there came the Great Fire when a large portion of the city was devastated. Some time afterward it was observed that strange and exotic flowers which had never before been seen, sprang up in the vacant lots. Seeds which had long lain dormant in the cold soil suddenly sprang into life with the heat of the fire. The fire of God falling on a believer will achieve in ten minutes what he could not achieve in himself in ten years.

> 'Twas most impossible of all
> That here in me sin's reign should cease,
> Yet shall it be? I know it shall,
> 'Tis certain though impossible.
> The thing impossible shall be;
> All things are possible to me.
>
> —C. WESLEY

The falling of the fire *left nothing but ashes.* All that was combustible was consumed, only that which was indestructible remained. Fire can do no more to ashes. The fire of God will consume the carnal and superficial and leave only that which is of eternal value. Ashes have two characteristics. The slightest breath of wind will move them, and they invariably move in the direction of the wind. The life on which the fire of God has fallen will be especially sensitive to the promptings of the Holy Spirit and will always move in the direction of God's will.

> O Thou who camest from above
>   The pure celestial fire to impart,
> Kindle a flame of sacred love
>   On the mean altar of my heart.
>
> There let it for Thy glory burn
>   With inextinguishable blaze;
> And trembling to its source return
>   In humble prayer and fervent praise.
>
> —C. WESLEY

THE MIGHTY DYNAMIC OF THE SPIRIT

"And made them to cease by force and power" (Ezra 4:23)

"Not by might, nor by power, but by my Spirit, saith the Lord" (Zechariah 4:6)

READING: Ezra 4:1-24; Zech. 4:1-10

THE PATRIOTIC REMNANT OF ISRAEL had returned to Jerusalem from their exile in Babylon. They carried with them a decree of King Cyrus authorizing the rebuilding of the temple, and work on the project had begun with great enthusiasm. They had not progressed far, however, before they encountered organized opposition. By guile and falsehood adversaries had secured a counterdecree from Artaxerxes King of Persia, ordering that the work cease forthwith. Armed with this document, the exultant enemies went in haste to the Jews at Jerusalem and by force and power made the work to cease (Ezra 4: 20-24).

Discouraged and disheartened by this unexpected turn of events, instead of calling on the God who had so magnificently prospered their expedition, the patriots spiritlessly threw up the sponge. "Then ceased the work on the house of God unto the second year of the reign of Darius." The first round had been won by the adversaries of God and Israel.

It would be easy to condemn their lack of spirit and lack of confidence in God, were we unfamiliar with the intricacy and treachery of our own hearts. Under less testing circumstances we have doubtless made no better showing.

THREE CRIPPLING HANDICAPS

The Jews were working under crippling handicaps. They were confronted with *the antagonism of neighboring races* who had the ear of the king. The advantage was with them. They varied their tactics to suit the changing situation. First, *infiltration*. "Let us build with you." When this failed they tried *discouragement*. "They discouraged them." Then *intimidation*. "They made them afraid to build." Not content with this they aimed to produce *frustration*. They "hired counselors against them, to frustrate their purpose." And lastly, they wrote an *accusation* against them (Ezra 4:1-6).

How familiar these tactics of the adversary seem in the semi-totalitarian world of our own day. Incidentals have changed but the pattern remains constant. Christian minorities the world around encounter similar opposition in their struggle to maintain their faith and testimony.

They suffered from *lack of resources*. In his proclamation Cyrus had generously ordered that the expenses incidental to the rebuilding of the temple be paid from the royal treasury (Ezra 6:4), but now Artaxerxes' decree had canceled this provision. Deprived of this source of revenue, they were left bankrupt of the financial and military resources necessary for their great task. Worse still, the noble and lofty ideals which had inspired their venture had faded, and they were becoming reconciled to their failure.

But the most serious handicap of all was the *disqualification of their leaders*. Their governor, Zerubbabel, though a man of royal descent, had proved a broken reed. In the face of the organized campaign of their adversaries, he had wilted. He was no Winston Churchill who, on learning of the defection of France in World War II said to his cabinet, "Gentlemen, I find this rather exhilarating." Zerubbabel began well but did not display staying power and gave no inspiration to his discouraged people.

Joshua the high priest, the spiritual leader of the nation, was doubtless the holiest man of his day. Yet in Zechariah 3:3 he is seen standing before God "clothed with filthy garments" and consequently disqualified to minister on their behalf before God. Finding themselves without effective leadership, either temporal or spiritual, it is little wonder that the difficulties loomed before the people as an impassable mountain (Zech. 4:7).

THE VISION OF HOPE

Just at this critical juncture a message of hope comes to Zechariah in the form of a vision. Was it mere coincidence or by Divine ordering that the phrase used by the angel in the vision was the very one used by Ezra to recount the manner in which the work had been halted? Had work on the house of God been stopped by the "force and power" of their enemies? That was no reason for them to lose heart. "The hands of Zerubbabel have laid the foundation of this house; his hands shall also finish it" (Zech. 4:9). It would be achieved, however, "not by might, nor by power, but by my Spirit, saith the Lord." Despite the virulence of the opposition, despite their lack of resources, despite the incompetence of their leaders, victory was assured so long as they followed the Divine strategy. Success depended on neither Zerubbabel nor Joshua; on neither human force nor human power, but on the power of the Holy Spirit.

In vision Zechariah saw a lampstand, "all of gold, with a bowl upon the top of it, and his seven lamps thereon, and seven pipes to the seven lamps . . . and two olive trees by it, one upon the right side of the bowl and the other upon the left side thereof" (Zech. 4:2, 3). The bowl which served as a reservoir for the oil was continually fed with oil from the two olive trees.

The primary application of the vision would not be missed by Jews familiar with the golden lampstand in their temple. They knew God had chosen their nation to be a light-bearer in the world. But in this they had failed dismally and the light of testimony was all but extinguished. In His letters to the seven churches of Asia our Lord clearly indicated that the function Israel had failed to fulfill had passed over to the

church, and borrowing the imagery of the vision, we are
warranted in applying its symbolical teaching to the church
of our day.

THE FUNCTION OF THE CHURCH

The primary task of the church as symbolized in the figure
of the lampstand is to bring the light to a world shrouded in
darkness. What other function has a lamp? Responsibility
for reaction to the light is not ours. In the Revelation, Christ
is seen standing in the midst of seven lampstands, each of
which represented a living church, scrutinizing and apprais-
ing the shining of their lamp of testimony (Rev. 1:13, 20).
Just as the golden candlestick was the sole means of illumination in the tabernacle, so the church is the only medium of
light to a lost world. It exists to give light, and if it fails here
it fails everywhere. God has made no alternative provision.
"Ye are the light of the world," He said. And the light is
derived light, reflected from Him who said, "I am the light of
the world." How gross is the darkness of the contemporary
world! What idolatry and superstition, what cruelty and
suffering, what vice and crime, what materialism and cyni-
cism! It is in this very context the church and the individuals
who comprise it are to shine as lights.

But how is the church to fulfill its function? The vision
supplies the secret. The church possesses no inherent light-
giving power. Though illuminating, the lampstand was not
itself luminous. It could not generate light, it could only
bear it. It derived its light from a source outside itself.
Surmounting the lampstand was the reservoir, always full,
unfailingly pouring its supply of oil through the golden pipes
to the flaming lamps. The bowl in turn was kept full from
the olive trees which continually poured into it a stream of
golden oil.

The significance of the *oil* is clearly indicated—"My Spirit."
The church can give light only through the continual supply
and enabling of the Holy Spirit. The *bowl* would surely symbolize Christ who is the reservoir of all the Divine power and

resources. "In him dwelleth all the fullness of the Godhead bodily. And ye are complete in him," wrote Paul. The fullness of the Spirit is always at high-water mark in His glorious nature. Every needful quality for effective light-bearing is stored in Him and on His fullness we may hourly draw. He it was who poured out the Holy Spirit on His waiting people on the Day of Pentecost. "Having received of the Father the promise of the Holy Ghost, he hath shed forth this which ye now see and hear" (Acts 2:33). It is still He who imparts the same enduement today.

PROSCRIBED METHODS OF WORK

"Not by might, nor by power." The task of the church will never be achieved by purely human means. "Not by might, nor by power, saith the Lord." The phrase "not by might" may be rendered "not by an army," *i.e.*, collective power, force of men or of means. Sometimes it means "wealth," sometimes "virtue" in an ethical sense, or "valor." But in all its usages the underlying thought is of human resources.

"Power" here also signifies force, but rather the prowess and dynamic of an individual. It is never used in a collective sense. Taking both words together the phrase would mean that success in the church's task depends on neither the combined strength of men organized to assist one another, or on the prowess and drive of any single ididividual. *It depends only and entirely on the agency of the Holy Spirit.* And why? Because the task of the church is superhuman, and any resources of men and means, of skill and dynamic, are at best only human. If the task were only that of creating a visible organization, they might be adequate, but the church is infinitely more than a visible organization. It is a supernatural organism which can be nurtured and sustained only by spiritual means. The great danger faced by the church today is lest in the midst of careful planning and seeking improved methods, she forget the superhuman factor without which her task will never be encompassed.

Hudson Taylor placed great emphasis on this vital truth.

"The supreme want of all missions," he wrote, "is the manifested presence of the Holy Ghost. Hundreds of thousands of tracts and portions of Scripture have been put in circulation; thousands of gospel addresses have been given; tens of thousands of miles have been traversed in missionary journeys, but how small has been the issue in the way of definite conversions! There has been a measure of blessing, but where are the ones that chase a thousand, and the twos that put ten thousand to flight? . . . It is *Divine power* we need and not machinery. If the tens or hundreds we now reach daily are not being won to Christ, where would be the gain in machinery that would enable us to reach double that number?"

The Jewish patriots had to learn that success depended not on absence of opposition, not on clever leadership, not on human resources, but on the indispensable working of the mighty Holy Spirit.

DIVINELY APPOINTED MEANS

"By my Spirit, saith the Lord." If we wish to enjoy the benefits of electric light, we must obey the laws of electricity. We have the benefit of a power only when we conform to its laws. Just so, we will experience the power of the Holy Spirit as we abandon every other dependence and obey "the law of the Spirit." If we are to illumine the world's darkness, it will be only as we submerge ourselves in the Golden Oil, and allow the fire of the Holy Spirit to touch into flame the wick of our lives. The great need of the world is of lives incandescent with the flame of God.

In the vision, one factor indispensable to light-bearing is never mentioned—the wick. Yet without it there could be no light, no contact between oil and flame. The wick exists only to be consumed. So long as it saves itself there will be no illumination. In the process of giving light, the believer's life is gradually consumed. Each time Jesus healed someone, He was conscious of virtue going out of Him. It was said of Him, "The zeal of thy house hath eaten me up." We will never be, like John the Baptist, burning and shining lights if we are not prepared to be consumed in the process. There must inevitably be exhaustion in self-outpouring, but we have the compensating assurance that "though our outward man perish, our inward man is renewed day by day."

Power for light-bearing is not inherent in the wick; it has no illuminating power. By itself it will emit only acrid smoke and black smudge. It is only the medium between oil and flame. It cannot conserve its own supply, but is constantly dependent. It is always on the verge of bankruptcy. Withdraw it from the oil and the light becomes darkness.

In Old Testament times one of the functions of the priests was to remove with golden snuffers the encrustation from the wick, otherwise there would have been no clear shining. Sometimes our High Priest must use the golden snuffers to remove from our lives things which encrust and hinder the clear shining of the light. He performs this office through His Word applied in power to the heart by the Holy Spirit. Let us cherish this ministry, painful though it be.

It is by the dynamic of the Spirit alone that the church can fulfill its function, not by resources of intellect or finance or zeal. Propaganda, organization, and brilliance are no substitute for the Holy Ghost. New techniques and better methods have their place, but they do not dispense with the need for the dynamic of the Spirit. We will see success in our missionary work only when He has prepared the way for our coming. Where missions have flourished, there is evidence of the Spirit having been at work before the advent of the missionary, producing heart-hunger, creating expectation, causing disillusionment with their religions and persuading of the insufficiency of the light they had.

What is implied in the phrase, "but by my Spirit"? That in all Christian work the superhuman factor is of supreme importance. True, it operates through the human, but it is the human interpenetrated by the Divine as the wick is saturated with the oil which is the Holy Spirit. Then we will not rely on our argument or persuasion to win converts and build up believers in their faith. We will trust Him to manipulate circumstances and overcome obstacles in our path. We will expect Him to enable us to "finish the work."

What a privilege is ours—to have the flame of God consume us as we bring light to a world enveloped in midnight darkness! On reaching the shores of India, Henry Martyn said, "And now, let me burn out for God." He did—in six short years, but with an incredible legacy of achievement in Bible translation left behind him.

> And when I am dying, how glad I shall be,
> That the lamp of my life has been blazed out for Thee;
>   I shall not care whatever I gave
>   Of labour or money one sinner to save;
>   I shall not care that the way has been rough;
>   That Thy dear feet led the way is enough;
> And when I am dying, how glad I shall be,
> That the lamp of my life has been blazed out for Thee.

THE MISSIONARY PASSION OF
THE SPIRIT

*"Ye shall receive power, after that the Holy Ghost is
come upon you: and ye shall be witnesses unto me . . .
unto the uttermost part of the earth"* (Acts 1:8)

READING: Acts 13:1-13; 16:6-10

THE HOLY SPIRIT is the Executor of the Great Commission
and Administrator of the missionary enterprise. In the great
missionary manual of the New Testament, the Acts of the
Apostles, we meet His name on almost every page. The
history related is one sustained narrative of His activity
through the church.

In preparation for His approaching departure, Christ
promised a Vicegerent and Representative who would be the
disciples' Companion and Counselor. "If I go not away, the
Comforter [Paraclete] will not come to you; but if I depart
I will send him unto you" (John 16:7). On the Day of
Pentecost they exchanged Christ's physical presence for His
omnipresence in the person of His Spirit. From the moment
of the Spirit's advent the consuming passion and main pre-
occupation of the Lord began to be fulfilled. The promise
had been that when the Spirit came upon them they would
be witnesses to Christ (1:8). The fulfillment was specific.
"They all began to speak as the Spirit gave them utterance."
And their speech was mightily effective.

In the record of their missionary activity it is everywhere
apparent that the acts of the apostles—and of the churches
too—are traced beyond the human channel to the Divine
source. The main Actor is the Holy Spirit and men are but

His instruments in the achieving of the Divine purpose. From first to last the Holy Spirit is the prime Mover and chief Worker.

The Day of Pentecost marked two significant events in the onward march of Christianity. First, *the inauguration of the Holy Spirit* into His twofold office as Comforter and Enduer. As Comforter, He was imparted to His fearful and sorrowing disciples by the Risen Christ in fulfillment of His promise (John 16:7), when He breathed on them and said, "Receive ye the Holy Ghost" (John 20:22). The promise of the Son was of the Holy Spirit as Comforter.

The promise of the Father was the Holy Spirit as Enduer, and it too found its fulfillment on the Day of Pentecost. "Behold, I send the promise of my Father upon you: but tarry ye in the city of Jerusalem, until ye be endued with power from on high" (Luke 24:49). "And they were all filled with the Holy Ghost" (Acts 2:4). It was only as the vastness of the task committed to them began to break in upon their consciousness that the disciples felt their great lack of power. On this memorable day when Babel was reversed, God graciously gave them an initial experience of the Spirit's empowering. There, men were confounded because one language became many. Here, they were amazed because many languages became one. It was this epoch-making event which marked the real beginning of the missionary enterprise. The Gospel in one day penetrated a score of countries and was spoken in a score of tongues.

The inauguration of the Paraclete into His twofold office was accompanied by another epoch-making event, *the institution of the Church,* the mystical body of Christ, a living and irresistible organism. In the days of His flesh, our Lord in Person provided a perfect vehicle through which the Holy Spirit could bring to pass the world purpose of God. But now with the removal to Heaven of His glorified physical body, His mystical body, the Church, was to become the instrument of the Holy Spirit. Everything Christ did when on earth was done through the empowering of the Spirit and ideally this was true of His Church as well. The baptism of the Spirit had a corporate significance, for by it all believers of all ages were incorporated into the mystical body of Christ. "For by one Spirit are we all baptized into one body" (I Cor. 12:13). This body through its members was charged with the responsibility of bringing the good news of salvation to the whole world. The Gospel was to be preached "in all the world for a witness unto all nations" (Matt. 24:14). The power for this witnessing they would find in the enduement of the Spirit.

ENDUER OF THE MISSIONARIES

In His final utterance, the ascending Lord linked the advent of His Spirit with the bestowal of power for the effective world-wide witness which was His supreme objective. "But ye shall receive power, after that the Holy Spirit is come upon you: and ye shall be witnesses unto me both in Jerusalem, and in all Judea, and in Samaria, and unto the uttermost part of the earth" (Acts 1:8). Christ's words were fulfilled not many days after, when "devout men out of every nation under heaven" heard their Spirit-given testimony. The Day of Pentecost was a sample of which subsequent missions were to be a facsimile.

The specific manner of the fulfillment was clearly stated. "And they were all filled with the Holy Ghost" (Acts 2:4). This was not an experience confined to those of the pentecostal company, nor did it occur only on an isolated occasion. Peter, for example, experienced subsequent fillings as recorded in Acts 4:8, 31. The repeated emphasis on this subject throughout the Acts is significant, showing that these early missionaries took seriously their Master's command not to engage in their ministry until they were endued with power from on high. And this enduement is the essential missionary equipment today, for apart from the Holy Spirit there can be no effective witness.

The idea behind the expression, "filled with the Spirit," was not of a passive receptacle to be filled but of a vibrant human personality to be controlled by a Divine Personality. Passivity was out. Every faculty of the disciple was in fullest and highest exercise, but no resistance to the control of the beneficent Holy Spirit was offered.

It is noteworthy that the term "filled" as used in Acts 2:4 and Eph. 5:18 frequently carries the sense of "controlled." For example, "And [they] were all filled with fear" (Luke 5: 26). "Because I have said these things unto you, sorrow hath filled your heart" (John 16:6). These people were gripped and controlled by their fear and sorrow. Thayer in his lexicon says in this connection, "That which takes possession of the mind is said to fill it." We are filled with the Spirit when we voluntarily allow Him to possess and control our whole personality and bring it under the Lordship of Christ. When He fills us, He exercises His control from the center of our personality. He constantly enlightens our intellects to appreciate and appropriate the truth as it is in Christ Jesus. He purifies and stabilizes our emotions, fixing them on Christ. He reinforces our wills to obey the commandments of Christ. Rather than obliterating our personalities He releases and enhances them. In this way the Holy Spirit infused new life and power into the lives of the disciples to equip them for their tremendous responsibilities.

This enduement of the Spirit was the normal and essential equipment of the missionary and for it there is still no substitute.

ADMINISTRATOR OF THE MISSIONARY ENTERPRISE

As Executor of the great commission and Administrator of the missionary enterprise, the Holy Spirit is given great prominence in the records of the achievements of the early church. His authority at the commencement of the new dispensation was vindicated by His strange work of judgment in the case of Ananias and Sapphira. The sin of lying to the Holy Ghost brought on both of them the dire penalty of sudden death. "Why hath Satan filled thine heart to lie to the Holy Ghost? . . . Thou hast not lied unto men, but unto God"

(Acts 5:3, 4). God would have men know that it was no light thing to trifle with the Holy Spirit whom He had appointed as Executor of His purposes on earth. It is not without significance that the first word in the history of missions among the Gentiles is, "The Holy Ghost said, Separate me ..." (Acts 13:2).

His first administrative activity is in *the calling of the missionary*. In the missionary call the initiative is with the Holy Spirit, not with the volunteer or with the church. The paragraph recounting the call of Barnabas and Saul (Acts 13:1-4) throws clear light on this subject. "Separate me Barnabas and Saul for the work whereunto *I have called them*," was the message of the Holy Spirit. The Divine call precedes any activity of church or missionary. The church's responsibility was to let them go, to recognize the Spirit's appointment, and act upon it. It is worthy of note that the Holy Spirit selected the ablest men for His purpose, and the church made no demur. The responsibility of the missionary was to respond to the call. In the final analysis, judgment of fitness lay neither with the individual nor with the church leaders but with the Holy Spirit. Their part was to be sensitive to His leading and obedient to His command. The church did not vote on the issue. The candidates did not submit sheaves of testimonials. The missionaries were discovered to a group of spiritual leaders while in an attitude of prayer and self-denial they "ministered to the Lord." But it has not ever been so. Especially in the early days of modern missions, missionaries went out in the teeth of the overwhelming opposition or indifference of a church insensitive to the voice of the Spirit—mighty men such as Ramon Lull and William Carey. But though neglected by men they were not forgotten by the Holy Spirit who called them.

Then the Holy Spirit *sent out the missionaries* with the church as consenting party. "When they had fasted and prayed, and laid their hands on them, they sent them away. So they, *being sent forth by the Holy Ghost*, departed unto Seleucia" (Acts 13:3, 4). The fellowship of the church was symbolized in the laying on of hands, but the authorizing thrust came from the Holy Spirit who was the real Consecrator. The church dedicated and commissioned those whom the Spirit had already consecrated. Without the prior ordination of the Spirit, the laying on of hands by men is in vain.

The selection of the sphere of work was also the prerogative of the Spirit, not of the missionaries. The Holy Spirit alone knows the strategy of the Lord of the harvest whose interests He serves. This is strikingly illustrated in the journeys of Paul. On their first journey the Spirit guided the missionaries to Cyprus, on the sea route to Asia and the Roman world. Concerning their second missionary journey we read, "Now when they had gone throughout Phrygia and the region of Galatia, and were *forbidden of the Holy Ghost* to preach the word in Asia, after they were come to Mysia, they assayed to go into Bithynia: but *the Spirit suffered them not*" (Acts 16:6-7). The Holy Ghost alone knows which are the strategic centers and who is best fitted to serve there. Carey planned to go to the South Seas. The Spirit designated him to India. Barnardo felt called to China. The Spirit retained him in England. Judson's objective was India. The Spirit directed his steps to Burma. And in the light of subsequent events, how important it was to the missionary enterprise that they heeded His leading!

Asia and Bithynia were to receive the Gospel in due time, but for the present the Divine strategy was that the message should travel westward to Europe, whence would stem the great missionary enterprise. Europe was ripening for the harvest. The Anglo-Saxon race were to be the missionary pioneers, and five-sixths of all missionary work has been done through their instrumentality. Paul was sufficiently sensitive in spirit to respond to the Spirit's restraint. He did not press forward in self-will but drew apart to discover in prayer and consultation the geographical will of God for him and his companions. It should be noted that the expansion of the church and its extension to unexpected quarters was due to the constraint of the Holy Spirit rather than to the deliberate planning of the missionaries.

The Spirit too *determines the timing of the missionary program.* How very slow God at times appears to be. Why wait seventeen years from the completion of the events on which Christianity is based before fully launching His universal missionary program, and then why send out only two? Why so paltry a task force in the face of such appalling need? We have to learn that God's thoughts are higher than our thoughts, that His ways are past finding out. It is our part to heed the restraints of the Spirit and wait on Him for the revelation of His timing. We must learn that there is such a thing as the tide of the Spirit. He is working to a meticulously accurate timetable, and in our own spheres of responsibility we disregard His timing to our own loss and disappointment.

The appointment of fellow-workers is also in the sphere of the Spirit's authority. Saul did not choose his own fellow-worker—he was assigned by the Holy Spirit. Even the brilliant and deeply taught apostle was not sent forth by the Spirit without a more experienced and spiritually strong senior. The placing of Saul with Barnabas was no chance happening. Barnabas was mature, experienced, a "son of consolation." To his gracious gifts the Holy Spirit added the intensity, the fiery zeal, the restless urgency, the brilliant intellectual powers of Saul, who had long been preparing in the school of God. Together they made a wonderful blending of gifts. But even in a team so spiritually alert and gifted there later came a rift in the lute over Barnabas' nephew, John Mark (Acts 15:39). Even this regrettable incident was overruled by the Spirit, in that two preaching bands were created instead of one.

Another activity of the Spirit is *the leading of the missionary to strategic converts.* One outstanding example is the call of the Spirit to Philip to leave the thriving revival which was in progress in Samaria and in which he was playing such an important role, for "Gaza, which is desert." On the face of it this seemed the opposite of sound judgment. But when Philip in obedience to the Spirit's voice reached Gaza his arrival exactly synchronized with that of a vastly influential man in search of Christ and His salvation (Acts 8:29). It was the reward of his unquestioning obedience to be invited to explain the Gospel to a prepared seeker who embraced Christ on the spot. And through this convert, none other than Ethiopia's chancelor of the exchequer, the Gospel penetrated into that kingdom. Apart from the Spirit's intervention Philip would never have gone to Gaza, and Ethiopia would have remained without the Gospel. Every mission field provides similar if less spectacular examples.

One of the acute problems of missionary work is the pressure of the powers of darkness. At times these pressures seem too great to be borne, but here too the Holy Spirit is active in *empowering against Satanic opposition*. Elymas the sorcerer withstood Barnabas and Saul, seeking to turn the deputy Sergius Paulus away from the faith. "Then Saul . . . *filled with the Holy Ghost* . . . said, O full of all subtlety and mischief . . . wilt thou not cease to pervert the right ways of the Lord? . . . Thou shalt be blind" (Acts 13:9-11). He experienced the cooperation of the Holy Spirit in dealing with Satan-inspired opposition. The Spirit first imparted to him spiritual insight to discern the source of the disturbance, and then spiritual authority to deal with it. He boldly unmasked the nature, origin, spirit, and aim of Elymas' opposition, and solemnly invoked the judgment of God.

Then, too, the Holy Spirit *sustained the missionaries amid opposition and discouragement*, when the Jews in their hostility to Christ expelled them from their coasts. The strange sequel was, "And the disciples were filled with joy, and with the Holy Ghost" (Acts 13:52). They were lifted above their circumstances and were able to rejoice amid their trials. They found indeed that the Holy Spirit was the Divine Stimulus and Comforter.

It was the Holy Spirit who *directed the church in the appointment of its leaders*. It was not done by majority vote

"Take heed . . . to all the flock [of God] over which *the Holy Ghost hath made you overseers*" (Acts 20:28). It was He who assigned the pastors to the flock. The appointments were His prerogative from lowest to highest, not of the officers themselves. For even the humblest service within the church, the men must be controlled by the Spirit (Acts 6:3).

At the first church council in Jerusalem, the presence and *presidency of the Holy Spirit* was clearly recognized by the delegates present. His was the deciding voice in any matter of doubt. The chairman's wording of the decision of the council was clear indication of the place accorded to Him in their deliberations. *"It seemed good to the Holy Ghost, and to us"* (Acts 15:28). He was accorded the place of first importance in their findings.

The importance the early missionaries attached to the work of the Holy Spirit can be gauged by the care with which they introduced converts and believers to His ministry (Acts 8:17; 9:17). Paul traced the ineffectiveness of the twelve men at Ephesus to their ignorance of the Spirit's filling and empowering (Acts 19:2-6). Is there not a strong case for a very early indoctrination of converts on this crucial subject?

When the church and its missionaries concede to the Holy Spirit the supreme place in their planning and activities, we can expect to see spectacular advance on the mission fields of the world. But the plain fact is that even where His prerogatives are not entirely ignored, He is afforded little opportunity to display His power.

It was otherwise with Jonathan Goforth under whose ministry powerful revivals took place in China and Korea. He was deeply concerned to see revival in his work, and with that end in view set himself to make an intensive study of the Person and work of the Holy Spirit. He then began to preach what he was learning to the Christian groups he visited. Deep conviction and confession of sin followed, and an increasing number of conversions.

While speaking in one Chinese city to a heathen audience, which filled the street chapel, Goforth witnessed a stirring in people's hearts such as he had never seen before. When speaking on the text, "He bore our sins in his own body on the tree," conviction seemed written on every face. When he asked for decisions, practically everyone stood up. Then, turning about, seeking one of ten evangelists who accompanied him to take his place, he found the whole band with a look of awe on their faces. One whispered, "Brother, He for whom we have prayed so long was here in very deed tonight." Everywhere they went in succeeding days, many souls sought salvation. They had conceded to the Holy Spirit His rightful place in the missionary enterprise and reaped their reward in His mighty working in their midst.

One of the most thrilling stories of the moving of the Spirit on the mission field is that of the Lone Star Mission in Ongole, India. After fifteen years of sacrificial work, only ten converts had been won and in view of a heavy deficit, the Baptist Missionary Union in 1853 were deciding to close down the station. Dr. Colver made an eloquent plea for the little church, won at such cost. Dr. Edwin Bright, the Secretary, followed with a speech which concluded, "Who is the man who would write the letter or carry the message to that little church of ten members, telling them that American Baptists had resolved to abandon them?" He strode up and down the platform saying, "And who shall write the letter?"

That night, Dr. Samuel Smith, author of "My country, 'tis of thee," could not sleep. During the debate a map had been hung, the mission stations being marked with stars. Burma was thickly studded, but Nellore stood alone in India. Someone had referred to the lone star. Taking pencil and paper, Dr. Smith wrote:

> Shine on, Lone Star, thy radiance bright
> Shall spread o'er all the eastern sky;
> Morn breaks apace from gloom and night!
> Shine on and bless the pilgrim's eye.

Shine on, Lone Star, I would not dim
　The light that gleams with dubious ray.
The lonely star of Bethlehem
　Led on a bright and glorious day.

Shine on, Lone Star, in grief and tears,
　And sad reverses oft baptized;
Shine on amid thy sister spheres:
　Lone stars in heaven are not despised.

Shine on, Lone Star; who lifts a hand
　To dash to earth so bright a gem,
A new 'lost pleiad' from the band
　That sparkles in night's diadem?

Shine on, Lone Star, the days draw near
　When none shall shine more fair than thou;
Thou, born and mused in doubt and fear,
　Wilt gather on Immanuel's brow.

Shine on, Lone Star, till earth redeemed,
　In dust shall bid its idols fall;
And thousands where thy radiance beamed
　Shall crown the Saviour Lord of All.

At breakfast, Judge Harris, the chairman, asked Dr. Smith his opinion. He produced the poem. He read it at the meeting with much feeling. It shook the audience, and men wept. A vision of hope dawned.

And the result? A great movement of the Spirit crowned their faith. In a single day 2,222 baptisms took place. Thirty years later the Ongole church had 15,000 members, the largest Baptist church in the world.

THE SPIRIT AND SPEAKING WITH TONGUES (1)

"They . . . all began to speak with other tongues as the Spirit gave them utterance" (Acts 2:4)

READING: I Corinthians 12:6-11; 28-31

THE PHENOMENA accompanying the descent of the Holy Spirit on the Day of Pentecost bore clear witness to the release of a new spiritual power, the dawning of a new era. The polyglot crowds were confounded by the spectacular gift of speaking with tongues bestowed on the apostles. They were amazed but deeply impressed by the fact that "every man heard them speak in his own language."

Speaking with tongues occurred also on two subsequent occasions when the Holy Spirit descended on Gentile groups in Caesarea and Ephesus. On this foundation of fact has been erected the great superstructure of what is generally termed the Pentecostal movement. The majority of adherents of this group of churches holds that speaking with tongues is the necessary accompaniment and evidence of the baptism or enduement with the Holy Spirit. The movement has experienced spectacular growth during the past half-century. In the United States of America it is the fastest growing of all church groups. This alone should stimulate inquiry into its claims and Scriptural basis. If we are missing some blessing which God has for us, we should know it. If the movement though sincere is mistaken in some of its emphases, we should know it.

Pentecostalism is not a heresy for it denies no doctrine of evangelical Christianity. Indeed, it contends earnestly for the faith. We must therefore bear in mind that even though

we may not agree with the views of Pentecostalists, they are
fellow members of the Body of Christ. That adherents of
this movement are mistaken on certain points we believe,
but many of them are utterly sincere and intensely earnest.
Pentecostalism may perhaps, without any desire to be offen-
sive, best be described as a spiritual infatuation. And an
infatuation is seldom overcome by cold and logical argument. To approach those in the emotional, almost ecstatic
grip of this teaching merely with a series of syllogisms, even
if supported by appropriate Scriptures, will generally leave
them entirely unmoved. They are in the enjoyment of something which they are not willing to surrender for what they
consider to be the cold and unsatisfying doctrine of many
evangelical churches.

May it not be that hungry Christians and new converts
have been driven into the arms of this group because it holds
out the promise of something more vital, more satisfying,
more dynamic than the type of Christianity they encounter
in our churches? As they compare the zeal and fervor of
the early church with the lukewarmness of most churches of
our day, have they not grounds for following something
which promises a repetition of early church power? Has our
teaching in this connection been inadequate or defective?
We do well to be challenged by the virility of the Pentecostal
movement around the world, both in its home ministry and
its missionary outreach.

THE PENTECOSTAL GIFT

What was "the promise of the Father" for which our Lord
commanded His disciples to wait in Jerusalem? It was not
the gift of tongues, but enduement with power from on high,
and these two things are quite distinct and separable (Luke
24:49). The evidence of having received the enduement
was to be effectiveness in witness. When our Lord amplified
the promise as recorded in Acts 1:8, He made it clear that
the result of the coming of the Spirit upon them would be
the power of effective and extensive witness to the risen

Christ: "Ye shall receive power, after that the Holy Ghost is come upon you: and ye shall be witnesses unto me . . . unto the uttermost part of the earth." It is true that this enduement was accompanied by "speaking with other tongues, as the Spirit gave them utterance" (Acts 2:4), but this was neither the gift itself nor even its most significant evidence, as Pentecostalists claim.

OTHER TONGUES AND UNKNOWN TONGUES

In order to meet this assertion, several preliminary questions must be answered:

Are the "other tongues" of Pentecost and the "unknown tongues" of I Corinthians 14 one and the same? It should be noted that "unknown" used in connection with "tongues" in I Corinthians 14 (A.V.) is not in the Greek. The A.S.V. correctly translates simply "tongues." "Other" tongues occurs only once—in Acts 2:4. In Acts 10:46 and 19:6 the rendering is simply "with tongues," and in the latter passage the addition of "and prophesied" would seem to make a distinction between ecstatic utterances and plainly spoken teaching.

In his commentary, E. H. Plumptre asserts that apart from the Day of Pentecost, the tongues were not "the power of speaking in a language which had not been learned by the common way of learning, but the ecstatic utterance of rapturous devotion." His contention has much Scriptural support.

> At Pentecost *all* spoke in tongues (Acts 2:4). This was not true of the believers at Corinth (I Cor. 12:30).
> At Pentecost the tongues were understood by all (Acts 2:6). At Corinth they were understood by none (I Cor. 14:2, 9).
> At Pentecost they spoke to men (Acts 2:11, 17). At Corinth they spoke to God (I Cor. 14:2).
> At Pentecost no interpreter was necessary (Acts 2:6). At Corinth speaking with tongues was forbidden if an interpreter was not present (I Cor. 14:23, 28).
> At Pentecost speaking with tongues was a sign or cre-

dential to believers (Acts 11:15). At Corinth it was a
sign to unbelievers (I Cor. 14:22).

At Pentecost speaking with tongues brought salvation to others (Acts 2:41). At Corinth it edified those
who spoke (I Cor. 14:4).

At Pentecost strangers were filled with awe and mar-
veled (Acts 2:7, 8). At Corinth Paul warned that if all
spoke with tongues in a church assembly, strangers
would say they were mad (I Cor. 14:23).

At Pentecost there was perfect harmony (Acts 2:1).
At Corinth there was confusion (I Cor. 14:33).

Since there is such a marked difference between these two
manifestations of the gift of tongues, it would be questionable exegesis to build a system of doctrine on the identity of
the two occurrences. If the "tongues" of I Corinthians 14 are
not identical with those of Acts 2, what were they? The
"other tongues" spoken on the Day of Pentecost were other
than their native tongues. "Each one began to speak in a
language he had not acquired and yet it was a real language
understood by those from various lands familiar with them.
It was not jargon, but intelligible language." The "tongues"
of I Corinthians 14 were ecstatic, vocal utterances, fervent
and rapturous religious expressions, not necessarily intelligible to speaker or hearer except through the gift of interpretation. This description would fit in with the whole
teaching of the chapter.

William Barclay comments: "This phenomenon was very
common in the early church. In it a man became worked up
to an ecstasy and in that state he poured out a quite uncontrollable torrent of sounds in no known language. Unless
these sounds were interpreted, no one had any idea what
they meant. Strange as it may seem, in the early church this
was a highly coveted gift. It was a dangerous gift. For one
thing it was abnormal and greatly admired and therefore the
person who possessed it was very liable to develop a certain
spiritual pride in his gift; and for another thing, the very
desire to possess it produced, at least in some, a kind of self-

hypnotism and a kind of deliberately induced hysteria which issued in a completely false and deluded and synthetic speaking with tongues."

But it must be remembered that this kind of ecstatic utterance is not by any means the sole prerogative of Pentecostalism. It is familiar to both Islam and Hinduism, to Mormonism and Spiritism. This fact alone should cause one to view with reserve any claim that speaking with tongues is the necessary and only evidence of the Spirit's baptism or enduement. One writer claims, "In nearly all religions at the point where fervor merges into fanaticism, there are similar manifestations." Speaking with tongues, then, may be the working of the Spirit of Error as well as the Spirit of Truth.

CAN THERE BE GENUINE "TONGUES" TODAY?

Two views are held on this question. The first is well expressed in the words of Sir Robert Anderson, stated with his characteristic conviction. "It is not a matter of opinion but of fact that whereas the Pentecostal gifts and evidential miracles hold a prominent place in the narrative of The Acts and in the teaching of the Epistles written during the period historically covered by The Acts, the later Epistles are silent with regard to them. The natural inference is that the miracles and gifts had ceased, and the Epistles of Paul's last imprisonment give proof that this inference is right."

Supporting the same view, Dr. G. Campbell Morgan wrote: "We must remember that these signs were initial, they were incomplete. They produced no final result. They were necessary to arrest the attention of Jerusalem . . . They were Divine, direct and positive, but they were transient, never repeated because never needed."

A reasonable case can be presented in support of this view, although it is by no means conclusive. In I Corinthians 13, which separates the cataloguing of spiritual gifts in chapter 12 from the instruction in the worthy exercise of those gifts in chapter 14, these words occur: "Whether there be prophecies, they shall fail; whether there be tongues, they shall cease; whether there be knowledge, it shall vanish away. For we know in part, and we prophesy in part. But when that which is perfect is come, then that which is in part shall be done away" (I Cor. 13:8-10).

Proponents of the view that the Pentecostal gifts and evidential miracles have passed away maintain that I Corinthians 13:10 refers not to the final consummation, but to the full revelation of God's truth which was reached in the writings of Paul. In Ephesians 4:8-16 which gives chronologically the last list of spiritual gifts, the miracle gifts are omitted. And even of the gifts mentioned, two—apostles and prophets —are now withdrawn. With the coming of maturity and completeness, the three special gifts—knowledge, prophecy, and tongues—have passed away and ceased, because they have fulfilled their purpose. They were needed only while revelation was incomplete (See Heb. 2:3, 4). These gifts were the accompaniment of spiritual immaturity, and Paul said in this connection, "When I became a man, I put away childish things."

So the argument runs. It rests, not on any clear statement of Scripture, but rather on a series of reasonable deductions. The writer has used this line of argument with some enamored of the viewpoint of Pentecostalism, but entirely without success. There are no categorical Scriptural statements to which one can appeal as the end of all argument. On the contrary, several unequivocal Scriptural statements can be advanced against it.

"Forbid not to speak with tongues" (I Cor. 14:39).
"I would that ye all spake with tongues" (I Cor. 14:5).
"I speak with tongues more than ye all," said Paul (I Cor. 14:18).

In the face of such clear statements, to class *all* speaking with tongues in the present as spurious, "nothing but jargon and hysteria," would be rather sweeping and would hardly carry conviction with believers who hear in the inspired writings of Paul the voice of the Holy Spirit.

That most modern speaking with tongues may justly be classed as jargon and hysteria is not denied. Its fruits have not proved in the main to be the fruit of the Spirit. Even when interpertations are given, the subject matter is often puerile and adds nothing that is not much better stated in Scripture. Writing on this point, Dr. R. A. Torrey who studied deeply the early development of this movement, while believing that much of it was spurious, said, "We do not deny the possibility of God's giving a man in our day the gift of tongues." When the movement was just gathering momentum, Rev. George W. Soltau, a reliable Bible expositor, wrote, "Then is there no such thing as speaking with tongues? Verily there is . . . To whom has it been given? It would appear from such information as is at hand, that the real blessing has been given *in private*, often unexpectedly and without any seeking for it, and that it has been bestowed for the purposes of worship and adoration, not for soul-winning and display. There are some few cases of such gift being bestowed in public meetings, and such have been accompanied by a spirit of gentleness, humility, sobriety, and love."

The writer has personally known such a case as that referred to, when the manifestation came in private and unsought, and resulted in worship and adoration. After a few occurrences it ceased and never recurred.

THE SPIRIT AND SPEAKING WITH
TONGUES (2)

"Do all speak with tongues?" (I Cor. 12:30)

READING: I Corinthians 14:1-33

EVIDENCE OF BAPTISM OF THE HOLY SPIRIT

THE MAJORITY of Pentecostalists hold the view that speaking with tongues is the essential evidence of the baptism or enduement of the Spirit. They contend that without this manifestation the baptism of the Spirit has not been experienced or His fullness bestowed, but only a measure of the Spirit's presence and power. This belief is based on the fact that at Jerusalem on the Day of Pentecost, at Caesarea in the house of Cornelius, and at the church gathering at Ephesus the baptism of the Spirit was evidenced by speaking with tongues (Acts 2:4; 10:46; 19:6). It is of interest to note the cases in the Book of Acts in which there is no question of this experience having such accompanying manifestations.

A study of the three occurrences mentioned reveals that in each case there was a significant reason for the bestowal of the gift of speaking with tongues.

At Pentecost the urgency and emergency of the occasion was the reason. The feast of Pentecost had drawn a great company of Jews from the surrounding nations. Many were about to return home. With the crucifixion, resurrection, and ascension of Christ now in the past, the foundation facts of the Gospel were complete. The descent of the Spirit with the accompanying manifestations had aroused the interest of the whole city. If the immense crowd was to be evangelized, if the explanation of these significant events was ever to reach them, it must be now. Without the gift of tongues the witness could not have reached the men of these fifteen nations because of the language barrier. So in the exercise of His sovereign will, the Holy Spirit bestowed the gift, and the Divine purpose of the initial evangelization of these nations was achieved. There is no record of an identical repetition on any subsequent occasion.

At Caesarea the reason was different. The speaking with tongues was rendered necessary by the reluctance of Peter to obey the Lord's command to take the Gospel to Cornelius the Gentile. His attitude was exactly representative of that of the church at Jerusalem. In order to convince both Peter and the church that God had bestowed the identical gift on the Gentiles as on the Jews, God graciously gave a repetition of the manifestation at Jerusalem, but without its polyglot languages or evangelistic implications.

At Ephesus the Jewish brethren had heard nothing of the subsequent history of the movement which began with John the Baptist, and in which they had participated. They did not know all the facts of redemption or of the gift of the Holy Spirit. But through Paul's teaching their experience was linked with that of the church at Jerusalem and with the firstfruits from among the Gentiles at Caesarea by the same evidential gift of tongues, but again without the evangelistic accompaniments of Pentecost.

It would appear then that the purpose of the gift of tongues in these cases was not as evidence of the gift or fullness of the Holy Spirit but of the identity of the blessing bestowed on each of these occasions. It is noteworthy, too, that at Jerusalem, Caesarea, and Ephesus, *the gift was bestowed without being sought or expected, and in each case at one and the same meeting*. There is no precedent here for the "tarrying meetings" which have characterized the Pentecostal churches. The gift was bestowed in each case on the assembled company, not on selected or specially prepared individuals.

For the above reasons it cannot be maintained on the strength of these passages that speaking with tongues is the sole evidence of the Spirit's baptism and enduement. If this were the case, its practical effect would be to make it the most important of all spiritual gifts and, therefore, to be sought above all others. Paul's emphasis, however, is in exactly the opposite direction. Prophecy is everywhere given precedence over tongues, which gift he classes as of least importance. He exhorts the Corinthian believers to "covet earnestly the best [greater, A.S.V.] gifts," thus indicating that some spiritual gifts are greater and more to be desired than others. While positively urging the Corinthians to earnestly desire to prophesy, he says concerning tongues that they are not to be forbidden. Of no gift does he point out more clearly the possibility of abuse, and no other gift is so hedged around with restrictions and regulations. "In the church," he said, "I had rather speak five words with my understanding, that by my voice I might teach others also, in order to instruct others, than ten thousand words in an unknown tongue" (I Cor. 14:19).

THE PURPOSE OF "TONGUES"

It may be questioned, since this gift required such strict regulation and was so open to abuse and counterfeit, whether it is of any real value. The fact that it was bestowed by the Holy Spirit is sufficient evidence that in its pristine purity and when exercised within the Divinely sanctioned restrictions, it was neither unnecessary nor useless. If that were so, we would have no explanation of or justification for the gift of interpretation.

The gift of tongues attested the beginning of a new era and also served the important function of authenticating and confirming the inspired spoken word when as yet there was no written New Testament. God bore witness with His preachers by means of "signs and wonders, and with divers miracles, and *gifts of the Holy Ghost,* according to his own will"

(Heb. 2:4). It could also be the genuine expression of devotion and adoration and as such serve a beneficent purpose. We must be careful not to so exaggerate its inferiority to the other gifts as to impugn the wisdom of the Holy Spirit in bestowing it.

Rules Governing the Gift

While indicating that such ecstatic utterance need not be encouraged but should not be forgotten, Paul does surround its exercise with restrictive regulations. He did not question the reality of the gift but he was well aware of its dangers, for ecstasy and hysteria and self-hypnotism are very difficult to distinguish. If it be conceded that there may be genuine speaking with tongues today, it must be accepted as a corollary that its genuineness will be attested by its conformity to the requirements of Scripture. It was permitted on the understanding that everything was to be done "decently and in order" (I Cor. 14:40). From Paul's instructions the following facts emerge:

> The bestowal of all spiritual gifts is the sovereign prerogative of the Holy Spirit (I Cor. 12:11). Therefore no such gift can be demanded as of right. We cannot dictate to Him which spiritual gift we shall have.

> We are urged to desire earnestly the greater gifts, that is, those most to the edification of the church (I Cor. 14:12). The Corinthian church disregarded this counsel and majored in the spectacular, to its own confusion and loss.

> The primary object of the bestowal of any gift is the edification of the church (I Cor. 14:12). If any professed manifestation of the gift does not do this, it is either counterfeit or being abused.

> If anyone desires to speak with a "tongue" in public, he must first ascertain whether it can be interpreted (I Cor. 14:28).

> In the church, speaking in a "tongue" was to be con-

fined to two or three, and each in turn. They must speak in succession and not all at once. Failing this the tongue was to be suppressed (I Cor. 14:27).

If the exercise of the gift produces confusion rather than order, that is prima facie evidence that it is spurious, for God is not the author of confusion (I Cor. 14: 33).

REASONS FOR CAUTION

We recognize those who hold these views as fellow-believers and many of them as devout Christians. But we must appraise the movement in the light of its fruits and possible dangers. One of its great dangers lies in its tendency to subordinate the primary and essential to the incidental and secondary. Exaltation of the spectacular tends to make the great central truths of Christianity subordinate to subjective spiritual manifestations and the experience which such manifestations produce. Any teaching which does this is at once suspect.

Several dangers confront this teaching:

Spiritual Pharisaism. Of course this is possible in any Christian circle, but it is a special peril in a movement which claims to possess special or distinctive truth. The claim that the gift of tongues is the prime evidence of the Spirit's baptism or filling, and that this gift is more in exercise in Pentecostal assemblies than in other churches tends to beget a superior attitude. One of their number once said to the writer, "Of course we live on a higher plane than you do." This may very well be true, but it would have come better from other lips. But in fairness it must be said that this attitude would be deplored by the more spiritual of their members as it would by us.

Openness to Counterfeit. It is an indisputable fact that of all the spiritual gifts, this is the one most open to abuse and counterfeit. The fact that heterodox and anti-Christian movements also experience this phenomenon is clear indication that the manifestation can emanate from Hell as well as from Heaven. Satan delights to debase and imitate all that is good and holy and pervert it to his own base uses. The physical and spiritual realms are very closely interrelated and it is easy to mistake the one for the other. Fleshly enthusiasm and excitement can easily be mistaken for spiritual ardor.

Divisive Tendencies. To one who knows anything of the history of the Pentecostal movement, this point needs little elaboration. Both on the mission field and in the homelands there has been a constant history of division, both within the movement itself and in numberless evangelical congregations. It is sad that this movement which considers itself the Holy Spirit movement par excellence, instead of being characterized by the unity of the Spirit, is noted rather for its divisive tendencies. In view of this, Paul's counsel to the believers in Rome is apposite: "Mark them which cause divisions and offences contrary to the doctrine which ye have learned; and avoid them" (Rom. 16:17). Not all Pentecostal groups cause division, and this verse should not be interpreted as a blanket rule to boycott these believers.

Emotional Excesses. If in our conventional religion the emotional element tends to be unduly suppressed, exactly the opposite is the peril of this movement. F. W. Robertson comments: "The Holy Ghost may mingle with man in three ways—with his body, and then you have what is called a miracle; with his spirit, and then you have that exalted feeling which finds vent in what is called 'tongues'; or with his intellect, and then you have prophecy. In the case of 'tongues' men felt and could not logically express that feeling . . . The clear understanding vanished into ecstasy; the utterer, unless he controlled them, was carried away by his feelings."

This state of ecstasy was so pleasurable, and so excited the admiration and emulation of others, that in the Corinthian church, with its penchant for the spectacular, it became the prime object of pursuit, as in the Pentecostal assemblies today. Instead of steady continuance in well-doing, they tended to spend their time exhibiting intense feeling, and this uncontrolled religious emotion overpowered reason and sense. Mere natural and animal feeling was passed off as spiritual fervor. The same trends have been present in Pentecostalism, not infrequently accompanied by grievous and gross excesses.

The late Dr. Arthur T. Pierson, who conducted an exhaustive worldwide investigation into the progress and characteristics of the movement, summarized the considerations which should govern approach to the subject.

> The infallible Scriptures and not human experience alone can be the ultimate court of appeal.
>
> The gifts most to be sought are those most to edification.
>
> All spiritual gifts that are genuine are promotive of peace and harmony.
>
> All true endowments of the Spirit lead to humility and docility of temper.
>
> Any gift sought for its own sake or for self-glory is a delusion and a snare.
>
> All undue human influence is inconsistent with the supremacy of the Spirit of God.
>
> Whatever has a divisive and centrifugal tendency is open to the gravest suspicion.

We need to be always on the alert to detect Satanic devices and counterfeits.

POSITIVE TEACHING ON THE SPIRIT

One question remains to be answered. *How can we best help those obsessed by this teaching and prevent others from embracing it?*

We should early give to all Christians to whom we have the responsibility of ministering, full and positive teaching concerning the work of the Holy Spirit, the significance of Pentecost, and how they may personally appropriate the Spirit's fullness. When souls turn to Christ we should take the earliest opportunity of leading them into such an experience. This important aspect of teaching should not be postponed until they attain greater maturity. It is this experience which will bring them to maturity. It is amazing how much spiritual truth a young convert can absorb. It is our conviction that if this were a regular procedure in our churches, there would be much less backsliding and more rapid advance in holiness.

Where believers have been drawn into the Pentecostal movement, or are attracted by it, special care should be taken to meet the situation in a spiritual manner and not with carnal weapons. A frontal attack would be much more likely to drive them into it than to rescue them from it. On one occasion the writer was invited to give a series of addresses in a church which was on the point of being split on this very issue. In the whole series he neither mentioned Pentecostalism nor made any indirect attack on the movement. Instead, clear and positive teaching was given on the Holy Spirit and how He could meet their every need for a holy life and effective service. The Spirit bore witness to the Word, and not one member left to join the Pentecostal church.

The method to adopt when others are being attracted by the promise of an experience of ecstasy and power, is to show from Scripture and demonstrate by personal experience that when the Spirit controls the life there is holiness and joy and power in witness. If we ourselves have never enjoyed the Spirit's fullness, our first duty would be to appropriate that fullness for ourselves. Then we will be able to demonstrate in practice as well as by precept what Paul calls the "more excellent way."

Paul's great hymn of love is not placed where it is in the Corinthian epistle by mere chance. Its lofty theme was introduced of set purpose, and its objective is clearly stated. "But covet earnestly the best gifts: and yet show I unto you a more excellent way"—than even spectacular spiritual gifts, the way of Christian love. The highest gift, unless motivated by and exercised in the spirit of pure love, is utterly valueless spiritually. "Make love your aim," pleads Paul, "and earnestly desire the spiritual gifts"—but not the one without the other. This is the "more excellent way."

EPILOGUE

THE NEW TESTAMENT knows three types of Christians—the spiritually mature, the spiritually immature and the spiritually decadent. It is tragically possible for the believer either to fall short of maturity or to fall back from it. The Scripture searchingly diagnoses the cause of such failure and prescribes its cure. The foregoing chapters are calculated to meet in part the need of each class and to show that satisfaction for every aspiration after a closer walk with God may be found in correct adjustment to the three members of the Holy Trinity.

It is for the spiritually immature to move on from an elementary interest in Divine truth to a full and deep experience of God in Christ. The panacea for spiritual degeneracy is found in retracing the steps which led to the failure and in a fresh appropriation of His more than sufficient grace. True spiritual maturity produces not so much a sense of having attained as a passionate purpose to "go on to maturity."

From the pages of His Word we have been awed by the holiness of God and His antipathy to sin. We have realized anew the beneficence of His providence and the discernment of His disciplines. We have been humbled by His infinite patience in perfecting Christian character and the promise of His strengthening presence in the midst of trial. Such a view of God is calculated to beget a holy reverence, a restful confidence and a comforting assurance that He is ordering our lives with infinite care and skill.

We have turned our eyes upon Jesus, have glimpsed His glory and majesty, the sublimity of His life and the triumphs of His death. We have seen Him impaled on a cross and seated high on a throne. We have heard His stringent conditions of discipleship and have envisioned the possibility of a life of kingly reigning through Him. We bow at His feet in worship and self-surrender.

Some of the supremely important ministries of the Holy Spirit have passed before us in review. His inspiring and transforming power, His purging and cleansing activity, His irresistible dynamic and missionary passion have assured us that He is one with Father and Son in their purpose to lead us "on to maturity." That life alone is spiritually mature which yields without reserve to the sanctifying influences of the Blessed Three.